MONA, ENCHANTED ISLAND

Gateway to Anglesey—the beautiful Thomas Telford suspension bridge, a masterpiece in design and one of the largest in the world.

MONA, ENCHANTED ISLAND

An Introduction to
Anglesey

—by—

Geoffrey Eley

MCMLXVIII

THE PRIORY PRESS LTD.,
Royston, Hertfordshire

© Geoffrey Eley, 1968

Published by

The Priory Press Ltd., Royston, Hertfordshire

The text is set in 11pt. Baskerville and the book printed by
Priory Printing Ltd., Royston

This book is
dedicated to my
children—

Juliet Elizabeth
Charlotte Bronwen
(born at Bangor)
and Richard.

Also to my many
Welsh friends about whose
enchanted land
I am privileged to write.

By the same author

'FARMS OF BRITAIN'
(in conjunction with Professor Sir H. G. Sanders)

'AND HERE IS MR. STREETER . . .'
'IN YOUR GARDEN'
(an edited collection of B.B.C. horticultural programmes)

Printed in England

CONTENTS

List of Illustrations

The author and publishers wish to thank all who made photographs available for reproduction in this book as follows:

Dust jacket colour photograph—British Travel Association

Frontispiece—Penrhyn Colour Service

Illustrations numbered 1, 3, 4 and 5—British Rail

Illustrations numbered 6, 7, 10 and 16—Mr. W. W. Harris, Conway

Also Mr. W. Evans (plate 2); National Museum, Cardiff (8); Illustrated London News (9); The English Electric Company (11, 12 and 13); Saro (Anglesey) Limited (14); National Library ot Wales (15).

INTRODUCTION

by The Marchioness of Anglesey

As far as Anglesey is concerned, the author of this volume describes himself as 'a foreigner', but those of us who live in Anglesey—as well as the ever-increasing thousands who visit us each year—will be grateful to Mr. Eley for this book, the first general work in English and entirely devoted to the island for many, many years.

It is not a guide book, though it does contain all the basic information that any tourist might need. It is rather a book to read through at leisure. Geoffrey Eley has included not only the physical aspects of the island—the unique geology, the rich bird and plant life, the mild, sunny climate—but also he has written about the historical and cultural background of its people.

Anglesey's part in Welsh resistance to the Roman and English invaders, the Tudor conquest of Britain, the story of the Welsh Bible, the 19th Century shipwrecks—accounts of all these are included. So too are a number of local legends and fairy tales, and the author deserves our thanks for keeping alive such material from a community's social past.

But this is not just a book of the past. Geoffrey Eley describes the Anglesey of today; modern farming and forestry, the the development of industry and the building of a nuclear power station, the vast increase in tourism. These things are certainly changing Anglesey very fast, but, despite the summer traffic, the caravan sites and the motels, I personally share with the author the view that Anglesey still has 'a sense of separatenesss'.

Even today the majority of the people are descended from a long line of Anglesey 'born and bred'; they inherit an ancient language and a living culture. What a relief this is in a world of mass media and uniformity. Mr. Eley pleads for this same spirit of individual concern and local flavour in Anglesey tourism. 'A menu of imported frozen lamb, with Italian cauliflower, Dutch potatoes, Swedish tinned peas and a chemically preserved mint sauce from London's East End is not Anglesey fare.' How right he is!

9

Such lively comment, even if controversial, plus a wealth of information, written against a background of obvious long devotion to Môn Mam Cymru makes this book very welcome to all of us who share Mr. Eley's love for Anglesey.

It is fitting that such a new book should be published at a time when preparations are well advanced for the official investiture, in a few months' time, of the Queen's eldest son Charles, Prince of Wales, at nearby Caernarvon Castle. On such an occasion great public attention will be focussed on North Wales.

Finally, let me say that I have enjoyed this book, and shall probably frequently refer to it for a long time to come. I am sure many others who read it will do the same.

Shirley Anglesey,
Plas Newydd,
Llanfairpwll,
Isle of Anglesey.

AUTHOR'S NOTES

Their Lord they will praise,
Their speech they will keep,
Their land they will lose,
Except wild Wales.

> ---*A Welsh prophecy about the*
> *fate of the Britons*

As Lady Anglesey writes in her Foreword to this book, the forthcoming official investiture at Caernarvon Castle of Charles, Prince of Wales, will focus renewed attention on North Wales quite apart from the visual splendour and historic nature of the ceremony itself. Few of the former Princes have been formally invested and none in Wales itself.

Anglesey and Caernarvonshire are very close neighbours in the Principality—at low tide in the Menai Strait it almost appears as though the island is part of the mainland. The suspension bridge between the two ensures an easy and free flow of people and commerce and yet the Isle of Anglesey gives both the visitor and the resident 'a strong sense of separateness'.

Before I started this book, the last 'general' work devoted exclusively to Anglesey had been published over a century ago, in 1833. It was based on a prize essay at the Eisteddfod in Beaumaris that year, and was written by a woman—Angharad Llwyd.

In her introduction she says: 'I shall combine so much of what has been generally made known through the medium of the Press, as to preserve the perspicuity and the integrity of my plan, whilst I shall rest the merit of my essay upon original matter culled from various libraries.' Apart from my own observations and studies on the island, made over a period of years since first being taken to North Wales on holiday as a child and finally living and working in Caernarvonshire,

I have—even as a 'foreigner'—received boundless help and encouragement to write the book from such knowledgeable friends as Mr. Dewi O. Jones, F.L.A., the Anglesey county librarian; Mr. J. O. Jones, M.B.E., at the time Secretary of Cyngor Gwlad Môn (the Anglesey Rural Community Council); and that prudent guide and mentor of the island's farms, Mr. W. Bowen Thomas, then county agricultural advisory officer. Like Angharad Llwyd, I too have been heavily dependent on the research and writing of scholars from 1723 onwards—and to whom the fullest acknowledgement is sincerely given.

I hope, therefore, that this book will meet a need; that it will help others to get to know Anglesey; others who, like myself, am neither Welsh nor an expert in any one aspect of Anglesey life or history on which, through the centuries, so many erudite volumes have been written, and moreover, on which there are in the island today so many qualified persons. There is, at the end of the book, a bibliography to help the reader anxious to go more thoroughly into any aspect of Anglesey I have touched upon.

For the purposes of this small contribution to the writings on Anglesey, I made Llangefni—the administrative centre of the island—my base, and without the friendly help I met there this book could not have been published and in this connection my further thanks are due to Mr. Dewi O. Jones for his careful proof reading on my behalf.

An increasing number of foreign students is now visiting Anglesey, some through the help of the Social Science Department of the University College of Wales, Swansea. They are finding as I did, that in few parts of the kingdom are there such enthusiastic librarians eager to help the scholar, as well as the casual reader, or few places with such a cultural heritage in literature as Anglesey and the mainland of North Wales. One of my colleagues during the time I was in the island was from Liverpool University, writing a thesis for his doctorate on the subject of tourism as a major island industry; two other students, from Budapest and Rome, were last year able to continue their research in ancient philosophy only with the aid of rare Welsh books sent them by Mr. William Flint, borough librarian at Colwyn Bay, where the library is responsible for preserving all books on ancient and modern philosophy under the national specialisation scheme.

In helping to preserve and encourage the island's great achievements in the Arts, tribute must be paid to the Anglesey Rural Community Council. It is about fifty years since this body was started to promote the welfare of country families through co-operation with other organisations engaged in 'advancing education, including the fine Arts, developing physical improvement, furthering health, developing rural industries, relieving distress or sickness, or in pursuing any objects which are now, or hereafter may be deemed by law to be charitable'. It is through the work of this Community Council that Anglesey now has annual county art exhibitions, music festivals and, since 1964, an Arts Fund helped financially by the local authorities, the Arts Council and the Gulbenkian Trust. The Community Council is active in literature, too, publishing a county magazine *Môn*, an Amlwch scrapbook, and a book on Anglesey folk lore; it is also planning to publish a series of stencilled handbooks on the parishes of Anglesey to help cater for a rapidly increasing demand from tourists for local historical information about the island.

In the recording of knowledge and making it available in published form I should also like to give the highest praise to the Anglesey Antiquarian Society and Field Club, under the presidency of the Marquess of Anglesey, whose *Transactions*, edited by Professor O. Ogwen Williams, of the University College of Wales, Aberystwyth, are of the highest importance to the student of Anglesey life.

Finally, in this book I have tried to kindle an interest in the people and customs, the peace and simplicity of this cultured island whose voice neither time nor social change have silenced. A steadfast, little Wales of its own.

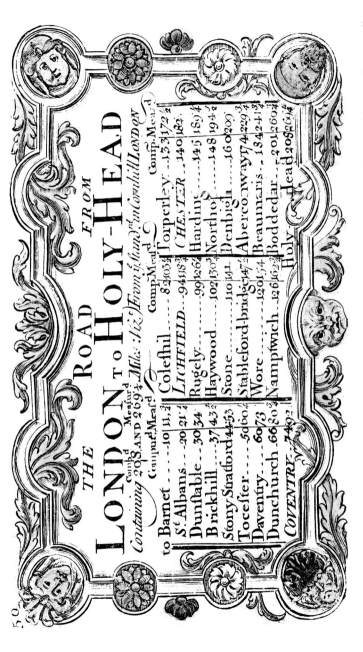

An old list of places on the post road from London to Holyhead—see also over page. Note he differences between 'computed' and 'measured' distances on the scroll.

The Island of MONA or ANGLESEY is in Circumference 63 Miles, contains about 200,000 Acres, 74 Parishes, & 1840 Houses, has 4 Market Towns one of which (viz) Beaumaris send a Member to Parliament. This Island now Anciently called Tis Tila Opaca, from the great quantity of Wood with which it was over grown, but now it is very bare of Trees, especially in the Parts of Western parts; The Principal Commodities of this Island are Corn, Cattle, Fish, & Fowl, of which it produ: in such abundance that the Welch call it Mam Gymry &c. the Mother or Nurse of Wales. The Air at certain times by reason of the Mists & Foggs that proceed from y Irish Seas is Aguish, the Soils Rocky & Mountaynous, yet affords Plenty of Grind Stones, Mill Stones &c. Gives Title to the Noble Arthur Annesley Esq. the first of this Family being Created Earl of Aug: 16 1661 & 3 to Charles 2 Chief Seate at Bletchington in Oxfordshire, and Farnborough Place in Hampshire.

Description of the Island from an old scroll map.

I

HISTORY

THE MOTHER OF WALES

(Môn Mam Cymru)

Can I forget the sweet days that have been,
When poetry first began to warm my blood;
When from the hills of Gwent I saw the earth
Burned into two by Severn's silver flood. . . .

(from 'Days That Have Been'
W. H. Davies, 1871-1940)

Bon, Môn, Mona, Ynys Dywyll, Ynys y Cedyrn. They are
all the same place, whether the name was given it by the
ancient Britons, the Romans or by later Saxon invaders and
the place is Anglesey, an island only twenty miles long by
about thirty miles wide, jutting out into the Irish Sea from
the Caernarvonshire range of Welsh mountains. This pastoral,
peaceful land—'Mother of Wales'—is shy; it is a land of
mystery—the Dark Island—but her modesty cloaks an
immensely rich history, considerable contributions to the arts, a
social lead in education and child welfare and scenery of wild,
untamed beauty. Of all our coastal islands it is the one most
'foreign' in atmosphere—and a place that everywhere gives
a strong feeling of age and history.

Anglesey has always been an island of poets, writers and
—perhaps because of vast, open skies and a 'painter's light'—
of artists. It was George Borrow (1803-81 and author of *'Wild
Wales')* who, when he stayed at the Railway Hotel in Holyhead,
found that even the 'boots' there was a poet and a critic of
some standing : 'In those days', wrote Borrow, 'there was never
such a place for poets as Anglesey; one met a poet or came
upon the birthplace of a poet, everywhere'.

Perhaps it is Anglesey's sense of 'separateness'—a place
apart—which appeals. How rare it is in a country like Britain,

15

invaded by various peoples in various times, to find such an area as Anglesey in which people have retained so much of their own blood, their own culture and language and their own way of living. In Anglesey—we call it an island but at low tide it seems almost part of the county of Caernarvon—there has existed for centuries a degree of individuality nearly unique in England and Wales, and until recent years more people spoke Welsh than in any other part of the Principality.

Against Anglesey, Anglo-Saxon and early Norman invasions failed; Scandinavian marauders made little or no impact; and it was only with Edward's conquest that English influence began to affect the island. Even then the only operative changes came about through English law, as it affected land tenure and inheritance. Very largely Anglesey was left to develop its homes and its farming in its own way, from the original Celtic settlements.

Its population has increased only by just over three per cent since 1931, and the density today is only one person to three acres. At the turn of the 19th century Anglesey, with a population of little over 30,000, ranked as the third smallest of all the Welsh counties. After this, the building of both the Menai bridge and the tubular Britannia railway bridge helped to put the population up—particularly in such towns as Holyhead, Beaumaris, and the areas around the Menai bridge itself —but even today the whole 275 square miles of island carries only 56,000 people—less than the population of just one of the smaller London boroughs.

Anglesey was called Bon by the ancient Britons, a name signifying an end, or extremity—which it is, off the northern tip of the Principality itself. It was called Ynys Dywyll, from its inpenetrable darkness of forest many centuries ago, and Ynys y Cedryn from its Druid heroes, but the generally used name until about the 9th century A.D. was first Môn and then Mona—the 'a' being added by the Romans. There are nearly fifty ruined windmills on the island, reminders that in medieval times it was Môn Mam Cymru, Mona 'the Mother of Wales', or Mona the Granary of Wales, since this island was then the granary for a wide area around. Giraldus Cambrensis, the 12th century chronicler, said of Anglesey 'when the crops have been defective in all parts of the country, this island, from the richness of its soil and abundant produce, has been able to supply all Wales'. The name Anglesey (Island of the Angli), came into use

The misty mountain backcloth of Snowdonia, Telford's graceful suspension bridge, Robert Stephenson's tubular railway bridge—all are seen in this panoramic drawing of over a century ago.

Lonely, fascinating Parys Mountain, once the world's busiest copper mine.

in the 9th century, when Egbert, King of the West Saxons, invaded Wales with a powerful army, desolated the whole country as far as Snowdon and then crossed into Mona taking possession of it after 'sore conflicte' with the Britons at Llanvaes, near Beaumaris. The island was, however, recovered by Merfyn Frych, a prince of Gwynedd, and the Saxons driven out.

It is a place of high winds, of golden sunsets across the Irish Sea, of wide beaches rich in coloured pebbles, of bird sanctuaries and of stone relics of a civilisation existing 3,000 years ago. None of this can be appreciated merely by driving from Bangor to Holyhead on the A5 road, or sleeping your way through Anglesey in the Irish Mail boat-train. Such travellers usually dismiss the island as 'unexciting, flat, barren and treeless', but this is simply not true. Granted, it is no longer—as it use to be— heavily treed, but woods of pine around Menai village itself have been cited as comparable to the beauty of the pines at Bournemouth, and woods or coppices surround many of the gracious houses of the traditional Anglesey landowners.

The feeling of Anglesey as a place apart was captured by Borrow, again writing about Holyhead: 'There stood I on the cairn of the Grey Giant, looking around me. The prospect, on every side, was noble: the blue interminable sea to west and north; the whole stretch of Mona to the east; and far away to the south the mountainous region of Eryri, comprising some of the most romantic hills in the world. In some respects this Pen Sanctaidd, this holy headland, reminded me of Finisterrae, the Gallegan promontory which I had ascended some seventeen years before, whilst engaged in battling the Pope with the sword of the gospel in his favourite territory. Both are bold, bluff headlands looking to the west, both have huge rocks in their vicinity, rising from the bosom of the brine.

'For a time as I stood on the cairn, I almost imagined myself on the Gallegan hill; much the same scenery presented itself as there, and a sun equally fierce struck upon my head as that which assailed it on the Gallegan hill. For a time all my thoughts were of Spain. It was not long, however, before I bethought me that my lot was now in a different region, that I had done with Spain forever, after doing for her all that lay in the power of a lone man, who had never in this world anything to depend upon, but God and his own slight strength. Yes, I had done with Spain, and was now in Wales; and after a slight sigh, my

17

B

thoughts became all intensely Welsh. I thought on the old times when Mona was the grand seat of Druidical superstition, when adoration was paid to Dwy Fawr, and Dwy Fach, the sole survivors of the apocryphal Deluge; to Hu the Mighty and his plough; to Ceridwen and her cauldron; to Andra the Horrible; to Wyn ap Nudd, Lord of Unknown, and to Beli, Emperor of the Sun. I thought on the times when the Beal fire blazed on this height, on the neighbouring promontory, on the cope-stone of Eryri, and on every high hill throughout Britain on the first of May. I thought on the day when the bands of Suetonius crossed the Menai Strait in their broad-bottomed boats, fell upon the Druids and their followers, who, with wild looks and brandished torches, lined the shore, slew hundreds with merciless butchery upon the plains, and pursued the remainder to the remotest fastnesses of the isle. I figured to myself long-bearded men with white vestaments toiling up the rocks, followed by fierce warriors with glittering helms and short, broad, two-edged swords; I thought I heard groans, cries of rage, and the dull, awful sound of bodies precipitated down rocks. Then as I looked towards the sea I thought I saw the fleet of Gryffith Ab Cynan steering from Ireland to Abermenai, Gryffith, the son of a fugitive king, born in Ireland in the Commot of Columbcille; Gryffith the frequently baffled, the often victorious; once a manacled prisoner sweating in the sun, in the market place of Chester, eventually king of North Wales; Gryffith, who, though he loved well the trumpet's clang, loved the sound of the harp better.'

If you go by road to see Anglesey you will cross Thon.as Telford's suspension bridge of 1826 which, like the adjacent Britannia tubular railway bridge, is both an engineering master-piece and a work of art, almost lacework in metal. This magnificent entrance to Anglesey took seven years to build and it comes on the last lap of the famous A5 trunk road which starts in the heart of London at Marble Arch, runs up through the shires of England, enters Wales from Chirk, on the Shropshire-Denbighshire borders, and finishes up at Holyhead port. This great post road of earlier times, previously called Telford's Highway after its engineering genius, is in fact virtually the route to Holyhead used by the Romans and later by the English in their march into the then wild and hostile land of North Wales.

Across the Menai Strait, the climate is soft, the air sea-fresh. There is a pattern about the Anglesey cottages, farms and homesteads both warm and friendly. The island is no longer the granary of Wales—grain can be grown better and transported easily from the drier eastern half of Britain, but the farms are well stocked with beef cattle, dairy cows and, today, very many more sheep than for a long time past.

Most of the villages and towns have developed around churches established in the 5th and 6th centuries. Some boast the longest names anywhere, such as Llanfairpwllgwyngyllgogerychwyrndrobwllllantysiliogogogoch, mercifully shortened for general use to Llanfair P.G., the village where the Women's Institute movement started life in 1915 and the forerunner of over 7,000 similar institutes in the U.K. today and of which Lady Anglesey is the national President. The full name of Llanfair P.G., translated, means 'The Church of St. Mary in the hollow of white hazel near to the rapid whirlpool of Llandysilio of the red cave'.

The only 'big' place on the island is, of course, Holyhead (population 10,650)—the island's only port and described by the poet Ruskin as 'that mighty granite rock beyond the moors of Anglesey, splendid in its heathery crest, and foot planted in the deep sea'. Holyhead with its mile-and-a-half long breakwater, behind which ships are so often glad to shelter, is the gateway to Dublin, and this gives rise to a strong Irish influence in Anglesey; and Irish money is legal tender. At Holyhead the great mass of rock torn off from the cliffs is called the South Stack and between this and the mainland the sea dashes thunderously in and out of dark caverns. On all the surrounding rocks and cliffs are hundreds of herring gulls, guillemots and razorbills.

Anglesey is a place of joy for the botanist, too. It has a large variety of soils, as well as an equable climate, and together these help to produce an unusually wide variety of native plants. It is also these conditions which enable gardeners and horticulturalists to grow many rare and half-hardy plants, some of which cannot survive in the open even in the warmest parts of the south of England.

Much of the quiet charm of Anglesey lies in the fact that it is, by comparison with most other places, still relatively uncommercialised. The island is set against a backcloth of the majestic mountains of Snowdonia, stretching from Penmaen-mawr in the east to the Lleyn peninsula in the west. It is a homely, friendly and unspectacular place of small fields and farms, whitewashed cottages and gorse-clad rocky outcrops jutting out in the middle of pastures which, in the bird migrat-ing seasons, attract whimbrel, golden plover, white wagtails and ruffs. Each of the rock formations on the island has developed its own kind of scenery, and this helps to give Anglesey its enchanting variety. Its setting across the Menai Strait is as lovely as, and not altogether dissimilar from, the setting of the small islands off the Yugolsav coast of the Adriatic.

The county town is Beaumaris (population, a little over 2,000); but the administrative and business centre is Llangefni, a pleasant, small town in the middle of the island. Anglesey itself is almost cut in two by a marsh—from near Red Wharf Bay to the sea at Malltraeth Bay—which is, in fact, a great furrow cut by glaciers in the Ice Age and running north-east to south-west across the island. Not all this marsh has been drained and is today a fascinating place for bird-watchers, the home of curlew, heron, redshank and kingfishers.

Anglesey is the only non-mountainous Welsh county, and in its interior are very delightful, reed-encompassed fresh water lakes, or llyns—again rich in bird and plant life, often covered with waterlilies. On at least one of these, on the outskirts of the family holiday town of Rhosneigr, bitterns can be heard boom-ing and, as noted by that great ornithologist, writer and artist, C. F. Tunnicliffe (who has made his home on Anglesey) so too at this lake, known as Llyn Maelog, one can see many types of migrating warblers.

Anglesey claims the title of 'the sunny island'. Sunshine totals for the months of March to October average about seven hours a day, and the 'season' begins about a fortnight earlier than that on the mainland. Apart, however, from its good climate (if you don't mind a blustery sou' wester wind off the sea), Anglesey is an immensely rewarding place for antiquarians, historians, geologists, naturalists, fishermen and yachtsmen. The yachting fortnight at Beaumaris is becoming a favourite, and the holding of the National Championships at Holyhead on two successive recent years has helped to introduce Anglesey to members of sailing clubs from all over Britain. At peak periods the Anglesey Tourist Association handles 1,000 enquiries a week from prospective holiday-makers of the discerning kind.

The future of tourism in Anglesey is a vexed problem; so is industrial development. The island is at a cross-roads in its history—it naturally does not want to be left behind, almost forgotten, in commercial advancement but neither does it want to lose its unique culture and dignity. The value of the holiday trade is at present over £2,000,000 a year and could well be four or five times this amount in ten years' time. To get this problem in focus, Anglesey County Council commissioned the British Travel Association, Britain's official tourist organisation, to carry out an on-the-spot survey and this showed that the island gets about 160,000 staying visitors in the season between May and September and well over 1,000,000 day visitors.

Peak months of Anglesey's holiday season are July and August, with 90,000 of the total staying visitors and 800,000 of the total day visitors. Where do they all come from? The survey gave the authorities some very useful and interesting facts, for instance that fifty-eight per cent of Anglesey's staying visitors and forty-three per cent of day visitors in one year were residents of Lancashire. A further twenty-four per cent of staying visitors and thirty-three per cent of day visitors came from other parts of Wales and the English Midlands—and a quarter of the visitors were on the island for the first time. The vistiors, questioned by the survey team, were unanimous that the most attractive features of Anglesey were its beaches and coastline, its scenery and quietness and its mild climate.

As a revenue-earner, tourism must undoubtedly be developed in Anglesey and the county council made a grant to help the Anglesey Tourist Association to promote the island. There are many ideas as to how this can be done without spoliation, enabling Anglesey to go forward to a life based on its traditional industry of farming but with tourism and a controlled amount (mainly confined to the larger pockets of population) of new industrial premises.

There is much to be said for the idea, springing from Anglesey's natural scenic beauty, of encouraging special-interest holidays covering history, archaeology, drama, music, ornithology, geology and outdoor painting, and there is an art centre at Beaumaris, in the old David Hughes school, which might encourage people to enjoy painting and sketching holidays.

It is indeed basic to the island's character as a nursery of writers, poets and artists that the arts should be a pivotal point in any plans for its future, and nothing but good can come from the decision of the Arts Council of Great Britain to run a North Wales Arts Advisory Panel co-operating with local authorities and others in ultimately establishing a North Wales Arts Trust. Another strong guardian of Anglesey's tradition is, of course, the Anglesey Rural Community Council who have been responsible, among other things, for developing the Welsh National Drama Festival, a county music festival, the Anglesey Arts Fund and innumerable literary, arts and music events and clubs.

Quite another problem is the industrial development of the island. Although agriculture is the predominant work of Anglesey, with an annual turnover of about £6,000,000 a year, not all the island's sons and daughters are dedicated to farming, but neither do they necessarily want to leave and migrate to Merseyside or elsewhere in a belief that 'the grass is so much greener on the other side of the hill'. Unlike so many areas, where industry has swamped up the land, its people and their traditions, Anglesey is fortunate; an enviable balance has, up to now, been achieved between farming and industrial development without raping and scarring the island.

Twenty new industries have come to Anglesey in about the last fifteen years and right in the forefront of these industrial changes is the construction of a nuclear power station at Wylfa. When work on this is finished it will be the world's most powerful nuclear source of electricity and set the seal on Anglesey's contribution to the national economy.

Great credit is due to the Anglesey County Council for its above-average enlightenment and far-seeing policies in finding ways of effecting the transition from the old to the new, and in their efforts to meet the challenge which inevitably flows from scientific and technical changes in a modern age they have the support of the government's recently-created Welsh department under a Secretary of State for Wales.

In February this year the National Trust announced the purchase of the Cemlyn Estate near Cemaes Bay on the north coast, from Enterprise Neptune—the Trust's campaign to save the coast. Anglesey County Council's gift of £10,000 towards improving the property represents 3s. 7d. per head of population in the area—the biggest *per capita* of any county council in the Neptune scheme.

II

TELFORD'S HIGHWAY

The three things that will make a wise man
—the genius of a Cymri, the courtesy of a
Frenchman, the industry of a Saxon.

(Triads of the Four Nations).

A part from boats, there are two impressive ways of entering
Anglesey. One, as mentioned earlier, is over the Menai
Strait suspension bridge, a world masterpiece in elegant
design; the other by rail from the mainland of Wales through
the iron girders of Robert Stephenson's tubular bridge supported
on rocks in the middle of the sea channel—this is the bridge
which more than 100 years ago earned for Stephenson the
tribute that he had 'done more to raise the value of property of
all kinds in Wales and to promote the social happiness of the
people than had been achieved by all its poets, statesmen, law-
givers and warriors since the Roman invasion'.

Before the road and railway bridges were built the crossing
from the mainland was made by one or other of the five ferries
along the Menai Strait. There was not much to choose in the
way of safety since all the ferries seem to have been perilous and,
indeed, the results of an enquiry into the loss of life by this
means showed that nearly 200 people died between 1664 and
1842 trying to reach Anglesey.

The road from London through North Wales and over the
isle of Anglesey to Holyhead has, like the Great North Road,
not only played a vital part in the economic life of Great Britain,
but also like other famous highways it provides the backcloth to
the story of human hopes and failures over four centuries or
more.

The first long-distance roads were, of course, those over
which the mail was carried by coach and horses from
London and other centres. As early as 1561 there is an official
record of a temporary line of posts—at each place with a post-
master in charge of the mail—from London right through the
mountains and lonely places of North Wales to the Port of

Holyhead. A permanent line of posts was established by 1599. From ancient documents we can gather than 'John Ffranceys was Poste of West Chester, Piers Conway of Rudlande, William Prichardes of Conway, Rowlands ap Roberts of Beaumaris and Robert Pepper of Holyhead'. A further new post between Beaumaris and Holyhead was started at Llangefni—in 1626, with Richard Roberts as Post Master.

The posts were usually at inns where the King's messengers could eat and drink as well as obtain fresh horses and guides to carry on their journey. The innkeeper was expected to keep in good fettle at least three horses for these messengers. He was also allowed to let horses for hire to travellers who needed them, a privilege which the innkeeper appreciated because the Government—and it was almost entirely for their purposes that the system was operated—was not always exactly prompt in making payments. The posting inns later became known as Post-Offices, the innkeeper became the first Post-Master and gradually the privilege of sending letters by mail coach was extended to the ordinary citizen. It became organised as a proper public service by King Charles I in 1635, with both a regular service of mail coaches and postage rates. In the case of private letters for North Wales and Anglesey and thence to Ireland, the ordinary citizens' letters were carried by post-boys on horseback.

The first accurate account of the original post road from London to Holyhead was published in 1675 by John Ogilby who had been appointed Cosmographer to the King. His work was called 'Britannia, or a Description of the Principal Roads to England'. The roads were drawn on scrolls and the maps were copper-plated engravings. The post road from London to Holyhead showed a distance of 224 miles leaving London via Barnet, St. Albans and Dunstable and, at the other end, leaving the mainland of Wales at Aberconway and entering the island of Anglesey at Beaumaris. This road—centuries later to become the famous A5—was called by Ogilby 'one of the six premier post ways and one of the most frequented—and affording good entertainment for travellers'.

The regular post road left Aberconway on the west side and eventually reached the sands and, passing under Penmaenbach, continued along the sands to the foot of Penmaenmawr. After this the track, for it was little more, led in a westerly direction over the Lavan sands for a distance of four miles to the edge of the Menai Strait opposite Beaumaris where the passage was made by ferry. The road could be used only when the tide was out. After Beaumaris the road ran westwards from Pentraeth (with its nearby gibbit landmark) to Bodedern and then, again when the tide was out, across the sands to Holyhead—described in the early 17th century as a scattered town 'consisting chiefly of houses of entertainment for persons bound for, or coming from, Ireland'.

At this period, without competent guides from Chester onwards the traveller could never be sure in what condition, or in what length of time, he would reach Holyhead. It was not until the turn of the 19th century that the time for a coach from London to Holyhead was reduced in good weather to about thirty-six hours. Either way, the delivery of mail in Dublin or in London was still dependent on a favourable wind across the Irish Sea.

The renowned Morris Letters record the arrival of Lord Londonderry in 'a hired chair and pair' in October 1743, an event of considerable importance in Holyhead. Ten years' later great excitement was caused in the same town by the arrival within two days of no less than eight coaches, chariots and post-chaises from Chester. By 1761 a lighter type of coach had been put into use and led to comments in the Morris Letters about the much improved prospects of travelling since 'flying machines, fixed to come and go twice a week in two days', were in use. The term 'flying' is, of course, relative; in fact these speedy models covered the ground at about five miles an hour compared with three by the older, heavier vehicles!

The next stage in the progress of the road from London to Holyhead came with the passing in 1765 of an Act of Parliament granting powers for widening the road from Porthaethwy to Holyhead, and charging fees for the use of the road. An interesting custom was that the Trustees sometimes 'farmed out' their business to the best bidder in an auction and the idea seems to have been to demand a price which showed a profit on the total tolls as collected the previous year. The tolls alone varied between £200 and £300, quite big money in those days. By the 1880s most turnpike roads in Britain had been freed, but it was another fifteen years before Anglesey's toll gates on the Telford road were abolished—the last length of road to be freed in the whole country.

The act of Union with Ireland in 1800 soon increased the traffic. With this increase came the inevitable complaints of the highway being inadequate and dangerous. Within ten years Parliament had appointed a committee to report on conditions and it was this committee which commissioned the famous engineer Thomas Telford both to survey the road and suggest improvements. After one or two schemes which were turned down, he eventually produced a plan for a suspension bridge over the Menai Strait. This time all went well and work began on it in 1819.

One witness before the committee, after studying the bad conditions of the Holyhead road, gave the following account of the Anglesey section · 'The journey of the mail coach across Anglesey (a distance of little more than twenty miles) is accomplished in *three hours and ten minutes*. I consider this rate of travelling to be quite unsafe on the present road, the steepness and length of the hills prevents the Mails from being driven fast *up* them, not faster than a very slow walk in some instances; the consequence is that the coachmen in order to keep the time drive at a most furious and dangerous pace *down* the whole of them with little or no regard to the rate of inclination, the narrowness of the road or the numerous bends in it; they let the horses got at the top of a hill and take their chance of a coach finding its way in safety to the bottom; that it ever does so is a matter of mere accident as the drivers have never, in such cases, any power over it. . . . Not very long ago the mail coach was overturned beyond Gwyndu going down one of these hills and a friend of mine was thrown a considerable distance'.

By 1822 the greater part of Telford's new highway was in use. Soon after, an embankment 1,330 yards long was built to carry it from the mainland of Anglesey to Holyhead. A new Half-Way Inn and Posting House was built at Caeau Mon, and called Mona. The building is now a farmhouse, but Mona is perpetuated on the milestones across Anglesey.

By mail route and over the ferry at Bangor was the way the author Swift crossed into Anglesey in 1727. He stayed a while at an inn called The George and liked it well enough. But there was trouble ahead. When he had crossed the island to Holyhead he fumed about the poor accommodation and the town itself—'a scurvy, unprovided, comfortless place'. Unfortunately for Swift, bad weather delayed the departure of the sailing

27

boat for Ireland for seven days causing him to write this
lament :
> 'Lo, here I sit at Holyhead,
> With muddy ale and mouldy bread;
> I'm fastened both by wind and tide,
> I see the ships at anchor ride.
> All Christian vittals stink of fish,
> I'm where my enemies would wish.
> Convict of lies is every sign,
> The Inn has not one drop of wine,
> The Captain swears the sea's too rough—
> (He had not passengers enough)
> And thus the Dean is forced to stay,
> Till others come to help the pay.'

It is from across the Menai Strait that the visitor travelling
overland has his first view of Anglesey, this green, gently-rolling
island of quiet villages and secluded beaches. Menai Bridge
itself is a compact little town situated beside a narrow and
lovely part of the swirling waters of the sea channel separating
the island from Caernarvonshire. Here each October 24 a fair
has been held for many centuries—it is called Ffair Borth, the
word borth meaning a gateway and Borth is the Welsh name
for Menai Bridge. From here, the first two miles of Telford's
road into Anglesey contain magnificent views of the whole range
of the Snowdon mountains, and the traveller soon comes upon
a striking Doric-style monument known as the Anglesey Column,
rising 112 feet from the wooded rock-strewn hill of Craig-y-
Dinas on the way to the village of Llanfair P.G. The work of
Matthew Noble, the column commemorates the first Marquis of
Anglesey who as 'Lord Paget' and 'Lord Uxbridge' fought with
Wellington as second in command at Waterloo. A bronze statue
on the top of the column represents the Marquis in Hussar
uniform gazing across the water towards Caernarvonshire. The
curious uniform, and the green stains which have coloured the
metal, give this statue an eerie appearance in certain conditions
of light and shade.

It is perhaps not surprising that someone found a way of
exploiting the full name of the village of Llanfair P.G. It took
the form of a printed sheet on sale in Bangor and Menai village,
giving details of a 'cure for Englishmen's lockjaw'. It is not
easy to understand why so many people thought they had lock-

jaw, but when they had paid their penny for the sheet, they found the 'cure' consisted of the full fifty-eight letter village name of Llanfair P.G. broken down into syllables!

Apart from the A5, or Telford's highway, the old 'post road' across the island is still there and quite delightful. Maybe it is three miles longer this way to Holyhead but it has its great rewards. The road branches off to the right from the modern road half a mile beyond Menai Bridge and very soon afterwards climbs the hill of Penmynydd—the place where the stage coaches and mails used to overturn. On this old road and about half-way across the island is Glan-yr-Afon where there was a noted inn, now, like so many others, a farmhouse. However, when it was still an inn, one traveller—a Mr. Hucks—recorded that he dined at the Gwyndy Inn and the hostess paid him and his companion 'the uttermost attention, and appeared particularly solicitous; gave us her blessing on our departure with a thousand admonitions not to lose ourselves'. After they left the warmth of the inn the rain fell and the storm winds blew to such an extent that later Mr. Hucks and his companion recorded how glad they were to quit Anglesey, describing it as 'this inauspicious island'.

Not long after the 1830s, and much as the old coachmen disliked the new-fangled idea of railways—they referred to engines as 'confounded hissing steam pots'—the days of the Anglesey coaches were numbered.

It was in 1838, at the request of the Chester and Crewe Railway Co., that George Stephenson surveyed a line from Chester to Holyhead. What was to be called the Chester and Holyhead Railway was incorporated by an Act of Parliament in July, 1844, and by 1848 there was a railway across the island. Two years later still, the Britannia tubular bridge was completed and the first journey by rail could be made all the way from London to Holyhead. Of the £2,000,000 needed to build the line from Chester across Anglesey, half was subscribed jointly by the London and Birmingham and Grand Junction Railway; the other half by the Chester and Holyhead Company. In 1856 the line was taken over by the London and North Western Railway and, subsequently, it became part of the London, Midland and Scottish Railway.

After leaving Belmont Tunnel, Bangor, the Chester and Holyhead line runs parallel to, but high above, the Menai

Strait and about a mile beyond Menai Bridge station makes a sharp right-angle curve and enters the Britannia tubular bridge 100 feet above high water. This bridge, named after the rocks in the Menai Strait on which the middle pier is built (and which were themselves so named after a ship which was wrecked there) is one of the engineering masterpieces of the world. It was built to carry trains weighing little more than fifty tons but which today, without any major alteration in structure, copes with trains weighing up to 600 tons. The bridge consists of two lines of tubing nearly 3,000 feet in length, and into its construction went over 11,000 tons of iron and two million rivets! On either side of the bridge tower stand limestone figures of crouching lions, the work of the Welsh sculptor John Thomason.

This tubular bridge was built on the same principal as the Conway tubular bridge—trains run *through* the girders instead of on top of them, and these bridges are the only ones of their type in the United Kingdom. In fact, according to the experts, there are only two others in the world—one in Egypt, and another across the St. Lawrence river in Canada. There may not be much to see from the rail passengers' point of view when he goes through these bridges but anyone who looks at the Britannia bridge from the line-side or some distance away must agree that it is indeed, like the Menai Bridge itself, an impressive piece of engineering.

The first station on the isle itself is Llanfair P.G. It is said that in the old Chester and Holyhead Railway days, when all its stations were small and not very comfortable, the one with the longest name was the worst. One night when the station at Llanfair P.G. caught fire it was deliberately allowed, on high authority, to burn down. So bad were the old stations that a local resident announced that not only should the station be rebuilt, but that in doing so it should be made a 'first-class' one—that is to say, with 'a booking office and a clerk'! More than once, practical jokers have removed the full Llanfair P.G. name from the station—on the last occasion dumping it in a railway truck which eventually turned up in sidings in far-away Berkshire.

Perhaps one of the best-known British trains is the Irish Mail. It is certainly the oldest named train in the country, making its first trip as the Irish Mail on August 1st, 1848—the day the line was opened from Llanfair to Holyhead. The actual train from Euston did not go further than Bangor, which was its northern terminus until March 18th, 1850, when the Britannia bridge was opened (before this both passenger and mail had to make the journey from Bangor to Llanfair by road, thereafter picking up the train to carry them on from Llanfair to Holyhead). By 1863, the down Irish Mail was the fastest train out of Euston and, unlike any other in those days, its daily workings had to be reported to the secretary of the railway company.

From 1848 right up to the outbreak of war in 1939, a watch carried in a leather case was delivered daily by an Admiralty messenger to the guard of the down Irish Mail. When the train got to Holyhead the guard's duty was to give the time to the captain of the Irish boat and afterwards the watch was returned on the up mail train to Euston from where it was sent to the Admiralty and, with great precision, adjusted in readiness for the next day.

Like Telford's Highway, the drama of the Irish Mail has for ever a place in history.

III

TOWARDS FREEDOM

'According to Plan'

(1210)

The King (of England) came to Chester.
Llywelyn then withdrew to the heart of
Anglesey after causing all the cattle and
movable wealth to be withdrawn to the
wilds of Snowdonia, and the king came
according to plan as far as the castle of
Degannwy. Then hunger struck his host to
such an extent that one egg was sold for
three halfpence, and horseflesh was as
acceptable as the choicest gifts. And for that
reason the king returned to England about
Whitsuntide, feeling greatly abashed, his
plan having miscarried completely.

The Chronicle of the Princess.

*(translated from the Welsh
by D. M. Lloyd)*

However necessary for the Anglesey visitor or student an
historical summary may be, topical events at this time
bring the story right up to the present day and from history
into the realm of current affairs.

With the forthcoming investiture at Caernarvon Castle of the
Queen's eldest son Charles, Prince of Wales, the grant for the
first time in 700 years of a personal flag for the Prince, and his
projected term of study at the University College of Wales,
Prince Charles will have closer association with the Principality
than his predecessors.

The design of Prince Charles' personal flag, devised by the
College of Arms and approved by the Queen, is historically
important because it is based on the coat of arms borne on the
shield and standard of Llewellyn ap Gruffydd, the last native

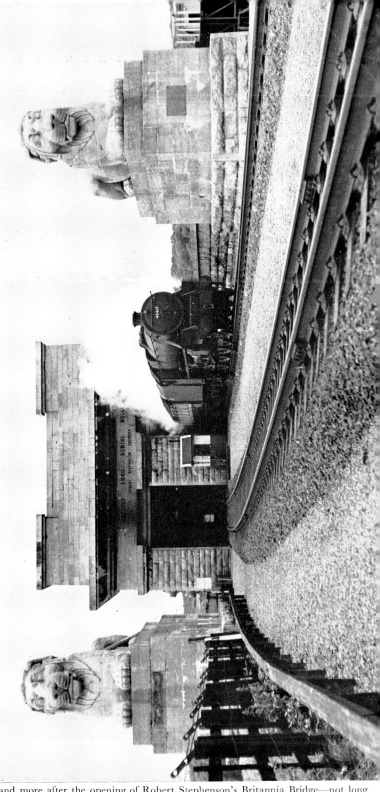

One hundred years and more after the opening of Robert Stephenson's Britannia Bridge—not long before the end of the era of steam and, with it, the last of such handsome locomotives as this. The bridge tower is flanked by stone lions by Welsh sculptor John Thomason.

The Irish mail train leaving Holyhead Admiralty Pier in 1908, with City of Dublin Steam Packet Company's steamers alongside pier. The tank engine on the train was changed for an express locomotive at Holyhead station.

Prince of Wales of royal origin. It consists of four lions in four quarters charged with the special coronet of the Prince of Wales authorised by Charles II (who had borne the title in his youth) after his restoration to the throne in 1660.

The crest of successive Princes of Wales has been the combination of three ostrich plumes, popularly known as the Prince of Wales's Feathers, with the motto in German, *Ich dien*— I serve.

With preparations under way for the official investiture of the Prince at Caernarvon Castle, it is interesting to recall that at the only precedent—of the investiture of the Duke of Windsor in 1911—there was no special banner devised for the occasion. Edward VIII, as he later became, was the 20th heir to the throne to carry the title of Prince of Wales.

None of the former princes had been formally invested in Wales itself. Those who had been invested attended ceremonies either at Westminster, or at Ludlow Castle. When Edward VII became Prince of Wales, he was the only heir to the throne to visit Wales before his accession since the time of Charles I.

The forthcoming events at Caernarvon Castle across the Menai Strait from the island throw into sharp relief the struggles of the islanders and the Welsh people as a whole, struggles which went on intermittently through many centuries before the final fight for independence against the armies of Edward I at the close of the 13th century when the Welsh were led by Prince Llewellyn ap Gruffydd.

The first major invasion of Wales—including Anglesey— was by sea, sometime in the third millennium before Christ, by people from the western Mediterranean. They were, in fact, the ancestors of the small, dark person one thinks of today as being 'typically Welsh'.

These early travellers went by sea to Wales because, at that time, what we now know as the English Channel and the Straits of Dover were either attached to the European Continent or, if there was a channel, it was probably too dangerous to navigate. We do not know why these Mediterranean tribes decided to settle and breed where they did, but of their occupation there are many archaeological remains.

Enormous stones, or megaliths, were used for building tombs for communal burial, and in 1910 a survey of these megalithic remains listed no fewer than fifty-four burial chambers in

33

c

Anglesey, of which about twenty now remain. What can be seen today is usually just the framework of the tomb, represented by heavy, upright stones, and above them the 'cap' stones. When the graves were first made, they were covered by mounds of earth, known as barrows, or with stones (cairns).

Geologically speaking, the most interesting of the megalithic remains on the island is the dolmen, or stone table, at Henblas, Llangristiolus. Two uprights are standing, one of them being fifteen feet high and nine feet thick, and resting against these is the fallen top stone—all of local Gwna quartzites. One fascinating thing about the top stone is that while it is rough on the upper surface its underside is ice-worn—so much so that even the direction of the ice movement can be determined. Knowing, as we do, that the direction of glaciation was to the south-south-west, the markings made by the ice prove not only that the stone has been turned upside down but turned round as well. Although the Henblas group is mainly natural as a whole, how the early builders, lacking all mechanical kinds of equipment, managed this job no one knows.

Generally known in England as dolmens, the burial chamber is still called cromlech in Wales—contrary to a recent dictionary of archaeology which states that the word cromlech is obsolete!

A big jump in time—to about 1800 B.C., the start of the Bronze Age. Then it was that a new people arrived from the Rhineland, known as the Beaker people from their characteristic waisted red or brown vessels of pottery. However, these Beaker people—pastoral and nomadic in their habits—left little trace of permanent settlements. The next important evidence of earlier inhabitants of Anglesey dates from about 150 B.C. when the first Iron Age Celtic people reached the island. When the air-field was being built at Valley during the last war over one hundred different objects were found in peat dug from the edge of a nearby lake. Nearly all these treasures, now safe in the National Museum of Wales, are of a military type. Among them are a bridle bit made of solid cast bronze; and another bridle bit which had obviously been made for driving a pair of horses, probably in a chariot. There is also an iron gang chain for captives or slaves, consisting of five neck rings joined by chains and having a total length of over ten feet. Other objects include iron swords and spearheads, metal parts of chariots and even a trumpet.

The Roman occupation of Britain left Anglesey untouched for quite a long time. It had become one of the last refuges, like Cornwall, for the oppressed Britains, but eventually the Romans did cross the Menai Strait in their flat-bottomed boats and were only stopped in their determination to conquer the island when they heard the news of the successful insurrection led by Boadicea, Queen of the Iceni. Anglesey was left in peace for a few years, until the coming of Roman forces led by Agricola. Here is a description by Tacitus of a battle at Menai Strait:

'On the shore stood the opposing army with its dense array of armed warriors while between the ranks dashed women in black attire like the Furies, with hair dishevelled, waving brands. All round, the Druids, lifting up their hands to heaven and pouring forth dreadful imprecations, scared our soldiers by the unfamiliar sight, so that, as if their limbs were paralysed, they stood motionless and exposed to wounds. Then urged by their general's appeal and mutual encouragements not to quail before a troop of frenzied women, they bore the standards onwards, smote down all resistance and wrapped the foe in the flames of his own brands. A force was next set over the conquered, and their groves, devoted to inhuman superstitions, were destroyed. They deemed it, indeed, a duty to cover their altars with the blood of captives and to consult their deities through human entrails.'

During the Roman period the islanders lived apart in the hills, occupying small circular or sometimes rectangular huts and these again are some of the interesting archaeological remains today. Some huts were built in open 'villages'; others were built within an enclosure of thick walls. The largest open settlement, consisting of over fifty huts, was on Holyhead Island, but later, partly because of continued Irish raids, many open settlements were enclosed.

At the time of the Roman withdrawal, it is probable that most of the Britons with whom they had been in contact had become Christians, and Anglesey has several early Christian-inscribed stones dated from the fifth century.

In the closing years of the eighth century great destruction was caused by Danish invaders, and it is likely that the cross which stands in the Deer Park at Penmon was put there about

35

the year 1000 to replace an earlier monument destroyed by the Danes. This cross has an elaborately carved rectangular base and shaft, with a circular head—embodying, it is thought, both Irish and Scandinavian design. Today, Penmon is the site of the B.B.C.'s Welsh regional transmitter, and nearby—at Llanddona—is the B.B.C.'s television transmitter for North Wales.

By about AD 950 Wales had much the same boundaries as today. Its people, who felt themselves to be the lawful possessors of the whole of Britain, had been cut off from other Celts by Teuton and other invaders from across the North Sea and the present day boundary of Wales was more or less marked out by the barrier called Offa's Dyke, running from north to south through the Marches at the foot of the Welsh hills. Laws too, began to take shape, mainly those of Hywel Dda, one of the kings of southern Wales. It was Hywel Dda who put the customs and rules of these people into writing, and although no original version of these laws exists there are several manuscripts written not later than the year 900 to give us an idea of the systems and customs of the Welsh people.

The country was divided into 'commotes' which were roughly equivalent of a parish and these commotes in turn were joined to 'cantrefs'. Within the commote people were divided into three classes beneath the king himself. These three classes were the free tribesmen who claimed connection by birth with the royal house of Cunedda and were a fairly large aristocratic body of men; the bondmen, or tenants of the estates; and finally the 'strangers'. But all were more or less nomadic. Even the wealthier people moved about with their flocks from the hills to lowland winter grounds; in the hills they had their special house—called a hafod—just for the summer period.

Whilst the English idea was to have a village centred around the manor, in Wales and on Anglesey there were neither villages nor towns of any sort for many centuries. The only 'planning', as it were, within the commote would be the Llan (a prefix to so many place names today) which was, in fact, an enclosure for the monks. The tribesmen's own holdings were isolated farms and only the cottages of the bondmen tended to be grouped.

Just as the commote was entirely different from anything in England, so were the Welsh laws and customs. Property was regarded as common stock to be enjoyed by all. They also had a very distinctive law of inheritance. In England property and possession normally passed to the eldest but the Welsh system—and it is one which has given rise to some of the characteristics and peculiarities of Welsh agriculture—was based on sub-division equally among all children of a family. This system worked well enough while there was still plenty of 'free' land to be taken over, but eventually it led to smaller and still smaller holdings incapable of providing a living. The only alternative was for one or more members of the family to renounce their share, leave the land and seek employment elsewhere—perhaps going to sea, or trying their luck in the 'foreign' land of England.

For several hundred years the history of the Cymry—a word signifying a strong nationalism among fellow countrymen —is confused, and fact is mixed with legend. The names of the heroes have remained with us—Trahearn ab Caradoc, Cadwaladr, Rhodri Mawr and his descendant Hywel Dda, and other holders of the lordship of Wales until the last great champion of independence—Llewellyn the Great, who died in 1240.

Anglesey has an important part in the story of Llewellyn for it was at Aberffraw on the island that he had a royal palace, a home for his princess—Joan of England, daughter of King John. Joan died in 1237 and soon after Llewellyn put himself under the protection of King Henry III and named the youngest son David heir to the Principality.

As the years passed the people of Anglesey suffered various vicissitudes and, just as the renown of the North Wales dynasty began in Mona, so it ended after more than eight hundred years in which they had resisted to their utmost all the conquering efforts of Saxon and Norman. They were soon to taste the unpleasant effects of rule from England under Edward.

Edward I did not foresee the restoration of the ancient British line to the throne of their ancestors. Here is a prophecy on this, said to be Merlin's, and published in Welsh and English by Thomas Pugh, in 1658, foretelling the troubles of the rebellion and the restoration of Charles II: 'Then shall a King come to England from a princely race, with his noble descent from Aberffraw in Anglesey, the ancient seat of the Prince of North Wales; then, or in such time when this cometh to pass, let the Britons sit still at home and be quiet, while the great ones of

37

England contend, for the crown shall go at the disposal of the subjects'.

It was on November 6, 1282, that Edward set out from Rhuddlan with the avowed intention of destroying the whole nation. However, when he arrived at Conway he heard of the defeat of part of his army and, having no other option, he turned back. Later, from Rhuddlan, Edward sent out summonses to the sheriffs of England to send all who were fit to fight to assist in repressing 'the rebellion of Welshmen'. On Anglesey itself Edward found no enemy to resist him. It is recorded that he 'builded there a castle and called the same Beaumaris as a check upon the natives of the island'. Already, however, much of Wales was in the hands of the Marcher Lords and it was only a skeleton of Wales that Edward subdued when, on the night of June 21, 1283, Prince David and his wife, two sons and seven daughters were brought prisoners to Rhuddlan castle.

The last efforts made by the Cambrians to recover the freedom they had lost came with an insurrection by Madoc (the illegitimate son of Prince Llewellyn), a revolt by Sir Griffith Llwyd and the rising of Glyn Dwr (c. 1359-1410)—more familiarly known by his Anglicised name Owen Glendower, an idealist and a mystic admired from Holyhead to St. David's, who dreamed of an independent Wales, an independent church, universities, Welsh as a common tongue and a culture different from, and more advanced than, the 'heathens' of a conquered country like England.

In a letter to Charles II, King of France, and translated from the Latin by T. Matthews, this is the plea Owen Glendower made for a Welsh policy :

'Whereas, most illustrious prince, the under written articles especially concern the state and the reformation and usefulness of the Church of Wales, we humbly pray your royal majesty that you will graciously consider it worthy to advance their object, even in the court of the said lord Benedict : . . .

'. . . that the Church of St. David's shall be restored to its original dignity, which from the time of St. David, archbishop and confessor, was a metropolitan church. . . .

'Again, that the same lord Benedict shall provide for the metropolitan church of St. David's, and the other cathedral churches of our principality, prelates, dignitaries, and beneficed clergy and curates, who know our language.

'Again, that the lord Benedict shall revoke and annul all incorporations, unions, annexions, appropriations of parochial churches of our principality made so far, by any authority whatsoever with English monasteries and colleagues. That the true patrons of these churches shall have the power to present to the ordinaries of those places suitable persons to the same or appoint others.

'Again, that the said lord Benedict shall concede to us and to our heirs, the princes of Wales, that our chapels, etc., shall be free, and shall rejoice in the privileges, exemptions, and immunities in which they rejoiced in the times of our forefathers the princes of Wales.

'Again, that we shall have two universities or places of general study, namely, one in North Wales and the other in South Wales, in cities, towns, or places to be hereafter decided and determined by our ambassadors and nuncios for that purpose. . . .

'In testimony whereof we make these our letters patent. Given at Pennal on the thirty-first day of March, A.D. 1406, and in the sixth year of our rule.'

From Anglesey down to Pembroke, the cause of liberty, freedom of speech and intense national pride had established itself. The people of the north and the people of the south united in loyalty to the leader Owen Glendower, supporting him in ten years of revolt. Wales won recognition from Scotland, Ireland and France and held its own parliament, at Machynlleth and at Harlech; even the English county of Shropshire declared its wish to conclude a peace with the land of Wales.

Owen was able to hold off the English, keeping them in their walled towns and castles. He even conceived a tripartite plan with two English nobles and supported by French forces, for the division of England and Wales into three parts—Owen Glendower's share to be Wales. This scheme came to nothing, however, and a little later the loss of Harlech, and with it his wife and possessions, marked the eclipse of this great figure. In 1410 he vanished. Owen's resting place is not known, but his spirit has never died. Sir Owen M. Edwards (1858-1920) wrote thus of Owen Glendower:

'But the common people of Wales did not lose their respect and their love for the leader in his day of misfortune. For years he wandered among his people and he was never betrayed.

Owain Glyn Dwr's career can be summed-up in two phrases—defender of the common people, and the incarnation of love of country. Love of country prepared him for his life's work; the common people's love for him, and their faith in him, gave him strength to pursue it from day to day. He drew his inspiration from the history of Wales; he saw the splendour, half imagined it is true, of her ancient kings. His letters to the king of Scotland and to the Irish princes are redolent of the dreams of a student of history. He saw the common people of his country writhing under oppression, enduring the tyranny of lordling and official, and with a keener edge on their suffering for having had a glimpse of a better life.

'He gave them a nobler ideal than merely that of hanging stewards and burning manorial rolls, the pedigree charts of their subjection. He gave a direction to blind resentment—national unity and a university. And no one has ever been loved as the common people of Wales loved Glyn Dwr is as if he were still alive with the nation, and it is no wonder that like Moses and Arthur, the location of his grave is not known. The poets sang their longing for his return, and the common people awaited his coming. They believed they would encounter him again on their way, that he would lead them to a higher freedom; they would not have it that he was dead.'

By 1536 Wales and England were one. The Act of Union, as it was called, decreed that English was to be the sole official language of all legal and government business in Wales. A Welshman who was ignorant of English was thereby disqualified from holding any public office in his own country. The Welsh system of land inheritance by equal division was discontinued. Parliamentary representation at Westminster was granted to the Welsh counties and county boroughs. However, unlike the later Acts of Union of 1707 and 1800, which respectively united the national parliaments of Scotland and Ireland with that of England, the Act of 1536 did not abolish a Welsh parliament.

Even so, the purpose of the first of the Acts of Union, as of those that followed it, was to bring about uniformity within the realm. 'Impelled by what appeared to them to be political and military necessity its promoters believed that a state uniform in speech and religion would be better equipped to meet the threat of foreign aggression,' writes A. O. H. Jarman in *The Historical Basis of Welsh Nationalism*. Mr. Jarman goes on:

'Another and quite different factor which influenced them was the prevailing view of cultural values. By this time the manners of London society had come to be regarded as the standard of civilisation, and the language of culture, in Britain and Ireland at least, was considered to be English. This attitude is well illustrated by the reference in the Act of Union to 'the sinister usages and customs' which still persisted in Wales. The lack during these centuries of a Welsh capital city, acting as a focus for the national culture, was an irreparable loss. English writers for the period frequently used the word 'civilitie' meaning thereby the qualities of urbanity and gentility of which London was, in their view, the obvious centre and source. Among the educated classes it was believed that this metropolitan virtue could be transplanted to Wales and, with tender nurture and a modicum of faith, made to blossom amid the quarrelsome squires and mountain farmers . . . the Welsh gentry heartily and unanimously welcomed the Tudor new order. To them as a class it brought advancement and increased wealth. London now became for a numerous section of them a centre of activity and a focus of interest, and for the remainder a source of social and cultural standards.

'Thus a millennium of Welsh history came to an end. A division now appeared in the national life, an ever widening breach separating the gentry from the common people. The crystallisation of landlordism into a social system and the Anglicisation of the upper classes proceeded simultaneously. Becoming increasingly alienated from its traditions and heritage, the Welsh aristocratic class renounced the duties and obligations which for time out of mind it has discharged and honoured . . . the common people were left to toil unremittingly, not merely for their own bare sustenance, but for the maintenance of a propertied class which was discarding all sense of responsibility for the well-being of a native Welsh society. From that period till today the main theme of Welsh history has been the effort of the people to recreate a society and to raise up new leaders to take the place of those who had deserted them.'

The sociological history of Anglesey, and the emergence in the 18th century of a middle class, was largely influenced by the farmers who formed much the most numerous group of the population, and was later added to by growing numbers of eminent scholars, lawyers, clergymen and doctors. So it was that unlike England—a 'nation of shopkeepers'—Anglesey's middle class was very largely an educated, professional one.

These professional men and their families, together with the landowners and farmers, formed, however, only a minority of the total island population. Most people on the island were not only poor, but were considerably worse off than their equivalent in England and many did not even have enough to eat. The Anglesey peasant lived almost entirely on porridge and a kind of cake or bread (usually made from either barley or rye) plus a certain amount of dairy produce, and on high days and holidays some goat's flesh—this was eaten chiefly in the hill districts and was cheaper than any form of meat eaten by the English poor. In 1739 a whole goat's carcase could be bought for three shillings.

The island's farms were, in the main, even smaller than the 45 acre average at the time in England, although there were some lands corresponding in size to the substantial English farm. They belonged to a group of men who would certainly not then have allowed themselves to be called farmers, but who were also distinguished from the bigger landowners by being called *Mr.* instead of *Esquire*. Few, however, seemed to have made farming pay well and as Lady Evans pointed out in her book *Social Life in Mid-Eighteenth Century Anglesey*, those families that remained on their land throughout the century, and did not replenish their resources from some new channel (probably one of the professions, or marriage with an heiress) seemed to decline.

Land was still cheap and plentiful—a farm and mansion house in the parish of Rhoscolyn was valued at £22 a year and William Morris' bride was described as an *heiress* to an estate worth £25 a year! Labour, too, was cheap and plentiful—early in the 18th century the senior woman servant in a gentleman's house was paid £1 10s. a year; the head ploughman on the farm £3 5s.

Notwithstanding the poor standard of living endured by most of the Anglesey population, there was immense enthusiasm for the education of children. Besides a grammar school founded in the 17th century at Beaumaris, and another across the Menai Strait at Bangor, there were plenty of country schools where, for less than ten shillings a year, a boy was coached in preparation for the grammar school. From remote villages a few boys went to university, and even if they did not they still strove in other ways for as high a level of learning as could be achieved and many were able to use not only their native Welsh tongue and English, but Latin as well.

Then, as now, Anglesey made itself a stronghold of Welsh literary efforts, and welcomed and encouraged others from beyond its shores, particularly—since it was then often easier to travel by sea than by road—from Ireland.

Another characteristic, if very different, feature of Anglesey life was Sunday games—in great contrast to the solemn chapel-going habits which were to come later. Wales, staunch Royalist throughout the civil war, had managed to avoid the first rigors of puritan Sundays and the day was still kept in Anglesey much as it had been in Elizabethan times. Once church services were over the afternoon games began—cock-fighting, quoits, tennis and the Sunday football. This football was not the kind we understand today, but was a variation, played between one group of parishes and another, in which squires and young people kicked a ball for miles over the country-side with the only time limit the failing light of day or sheer exhaustion of the competitors. There were similar football marathons in parts of England and at Ashbourne, in Derbyshire, the custom still persists.

Important cock-fights—particularly at Whitsuntide—were among the highlights on the social calendar which later came under heavy fire from the Methodists who considered such events as 'an invention of the devil'. Nor was cock fighting the only sport they put into this category. A Whitsuntide entertainment in Anglesey called the Interlude was strongly disapproved of.

The Interlude consisted of simple dramatic performances, usually depicting a few scriptorial or allegorical characters bearing a close resemblance to the miracle and morality plays popular in mediaeval days. Nobody seems to know quite why, but despite this apparent religious basis, the Interlude was not considered by Methodists to be entirely 'respectable'.

Gradually habits and customs changed, but not apparently without regret by some of the gentry, and even the men of letters.

One writer records in 1755 'that praiseworthy custom of nudging one another in fairs has been set aside here this many days . . . one may see lambs from Llanfiahngel Tre'r Beirdd,

43

Penrhos Lligwy and Llanfechell drinking together without so much as a hard word spoken, instead of breaking each others' bones like true Britons'.

The homes in which the people of Anglesey lived then and now are, of course, very varied. There is, however, a characteristic Anglesey home—humble but solid, attractive and enduring. These are the single-storied, two-roomed cottages built of stone and usually with whitewashed walls. They *were* the homes of the Anglesey poor. Some are still occupied by farm or quarry workers (no longer poor) but a lot have become comfortable, modernly-equipped middle-class homes or, quite often, homes of the Anglesey enthusiast be he full-time or part-time resident, geologist, ornithologist, writer or painter.

Here is a description originally written by Hugh Evans in Welsh in the late 1800's, admirably telling how the little white cottages came about: 'The *caban unnos*, a squatter's cottage of turf, was a hut built in one night, hence the name. If a man put up a cottage, if the name may be used in this connection, between sunset and sunrise and if he lit a fire on the hearth and sent smoke through a chimney, it was a recognized custom that he might remain in possession of the house although it was built on common land. Sometimes this happened when a bachelor took it into his head to get married and to set up house. His friends would gather at twilight and work all night to construct the turf hut; it was one of the conditions that the house should be complete with the chimney smoking before sunrise the next morning, and if there was time and labour enough a turf wall would be raised to enclose a garden. Hundreds of such houses were built, and hundreds were filched from the rightful owners by the schemes and trickery of the landowners.

'There were several of these turf houses in the neighbourhood of my old home, and when I was a boy I was familiar with the interior of four of them. They were inhabited at the time, and in one of them I remember a family of six children was brought up. In that particular house there was some kind of central partition which divided it into two rooms, and the father had made a low loft over the sleeping room as sleeping quarters for some of the children. All the children grew up to be well-respected and religious men and women and most of them lived to be a good old age. It is only about two years

44

since the eldest son and the second daughter died, both well over eighty. I never saw a happier-looking woman than Ellen Richards, their mother; her laughter was always ready amid the children and the smoke from the peat fire. The poor cottage was her castle and love transmuted everything into gold.'

By the turn of this century such *caban unnos* had acquired a cash value for farm workers, fishermen and Anglesey's copper miners of fifty pounds apiece freehold, or letting sometimes at is. 3d. a week (landlord paying rates!). It is difficult to imagine what the original owners would think of present day values.

On Anglesey, more than in many parts of the Principality, generations of families have retained the same Christian names for their children, many of the names coming from legend and history. For instance, the name Olwen was synonymous with *The Mabinogion*, stories of wild beauty and natural magic; Ceridwen was the goddess of poetry; Gwenllian a flaxen-haired girl and daughter of the powerful Madog ap Maredudd. If parents wish their son to be successful they call him Madog, a name which smacks of wizardry and violence.

Another fertile source of names is, naturally enough, from the great stories of the mysterious Arthur and his Knights of the Round Table. Arthur itself is a Welsh form of the Latin Artorius, but apart from what is an historic fact—the 6th century battle of Baden Hill in which King Arthur beat the Saxons—the name and the deeds of this leader of the Britons are at the centre of a web of legend which has spread through all Europe. So have the renowned names of Merlin and Guinevere.

IV

MARY JONES AND HER BIBLE

The Welsh Church is one of the most ancient Christian churches. When the original inhabitants of the British Isles, driven westwards from their homes, settled in Wales and other western areas, they took with them their religion, as well as their language. For 150 years or more, until Saint Augustine and his followers landed in Kent in 597 A.D., the Celtic church had virtually been cut off from other Christian practices, but this independence was eventually lost. The Church of Rome was supreme, and by the year 798 the independent Welsh church gave in to this supremacy, although retaining certain of its own characteristics.

Unlike the compact English village, usually grouped round the church, the Anglesey township is scattered and often the church is the most isolated building in the place. It is thought that this is in part due to the fact that the llan, or church, was often on a site formerly lived in by a Celtic saint who, having neither family nor economic ties among the people he was trying to help, therefore lived in 'a place slightly apart'. By contrast, when—centuries later—non-conformity became so strong in Anglesey and all Wales, chapels were put up in the centre of the towns, villages and even small hamlets. The first in Anglesey was built at Rhosmeirch in 1748 and by the turn of the century at least 24 Methodist chapels were erected.

The ground was already being prepared for this subsequent strength of Methodism by early travelling and independent preachers of the Gospel and by travelling teachers who helped the unschooled people to read the Bible in Welsh—the translation of which, published in 1588, had been done from the original tongues, in ten years entirely by one man, Bishop William Morgan born in a remote cottage at Ty Mawr, Pen-machno, in the hills of North Wales beyond Betwys-y-Coed—a village in which I lived while much of this book was being written. (Bishop Morgan's cottage is now looked after by the National Trust who acquired it from the Treasury in 1951.) By contrast with Bishop Morgan's intense application, the

46

English 'Bishops Bible' of 1568 had occupied the labours of nine clerics, helped by innumerable fine scholars of the day, for nearly ten years.

In Anglesey, as in the rest of Wales, the influence of Bishop Morgan's translation from the Hebrew, Aramaic and Greek texts was enormous. It increased the flexibility and usefulness of the Welsh language and contributed thereby not a little in helping to keep the language from dying. Bishop Morgan's work not only helped set a standard for subsequent writers of Welsh prose; it also provided the basis for a wide biblical culture far afield from his humble home at the head of the Gwybernant valley.

On Thursday, December 9, 1954 *The Times* wrote, in a leading article: 'The service which the Bishop of Bangor is to conduct this afternoon in St. Martin-in-the-Fields has been organised by the Honourable Society of Cymmrodorion to commemorate the 350th anniversary of the death of Bishop William Morgan, who translated the Bible from the original tongues into Welsh. The lessons will be read from the very copy of the first edition of his translation, printed in 1588, which he himself gave to the Library of Westminster Abbey; and its use today by permission of the Dean of Westminster is a pleasant link with the fact that it was the hospitality of an earlier Dean, Gabriel Goodman, which enabled Morgan to be in London to supervise the printing of his book. The occasion, however, will be something more than the celebration of one man's work. Those who attend it must perforce be aware of the national drama in which Morgan's translation was the controlling event, for the very fact that the service can be held in Welsh as a living language, understood by the congregation, is in a large measure due to him.

'Two events set the scene for the story of the Bible in Wales. One was the accession of Henry VII, a Welshman, to the throne, with the consequent attachment of many of the Welsh nobility to the Court. The other was the attempt of Henry VII to destroy the Welsh language. As a result the secular leaders of the people, both noble and middle-class, became increasingly Anglicised and out of touch with the common folk of Wales. To this add the Reformation with its removal of the religious leaders and forms of faith to which they were accustomed, and the Welsh peasantry were deprived

47

also of all contact with, and all interest in, religion. They seemed doomed to flounder in a morass of ignorance without guidance and without hope, and it was the Welsh Bible that rescued them, originally through the work of two Welshmen educated at Oxford, Richard Davies, who became Bishop of St. Asaph in 1559 and of St. Davids in 1561, and William Salesbury.

'It was Salesbury who first realised the importance of making a Welsh Bible available to the common people, and his advocacy is believed to have been largely responsible for the Act of 1563, which ordered the Welsh bishops to provide trans-lations of the Bible and Prayer Book. Bishop Davies trans-lated the Prayer Book and Salesbury the greater part of the New Testament, and the two were published in 1567. The literary genius of the Welsh had, however, till then gone chiefly into poetry, and little prose had been written for more than a century. If the Bible was to be translated successfully, the translater had in fact to create a new prose language, and it was that which the rather pedantic Salesbury failed to do, and which William Morgan triumphantly accomplished in his version, not of the New Testament only, but of the whole Bible, in 1588. The Welsh that Morgan wrote has been the basis of all Welsh prose since then, and his Bible, as revised by Bishop Richard Parry in 1620, remains (with comparatively few later changes) the Bible in use in Welsh churches and chapels today.

'The editions of 1588 and 1620 were Church Bibles, and it remained for the little Bible—Y Beibl Bach—of 1630 to begin to take the scriptures, with the Prayer Book and the metrical psalms, into the people's homes. Other editions followed, with slowly mounting results that in the end completely changed the spiritual and literary history—even the very character—of the Welsh nation. Indeed, it may be said that the effect was felt indirectly throughout the world, for one morning in 1800 a young servant girl, Mary Jones, set off on a walk which had great results. She had saved for six years to buy herself a Bible, and that day she tramped twenty-five miles to Bala to buy one from Thomas Charles, the pioneer of Welsh Sunday Schools, one of whose descendants is, by a happy coincidence, today Vicar of St. Martin's. Charles had none to sell her, but she wept so bitterly in disappointment that he gave her one of his own. Out of this incident—now firmly enshrined in

Welsh history—grew the foundation in 1804 of the British and Foreign Bible Society, which two years later issued ten thousand Welsh Bibles and has since issued Bibles in more than 800 languages. So when this evening representatives of the Welsh people give thanks for the work of William Morgan, they will surely have with them the thoughts of many nations more numerous, and of many tongues more widely spoken, than their own.'

In the years before the close of the 17th century a profound effect on the Welshman's home was also achieved by a book written by a vicar of Llandovery and called 'The Welshman's Candle'. It was a collection of religious writings directed at the need for moral integrity within the home if ever the reader 'wished to go to Heaven'.

The later progress of non-conformism was also aided by the fact that the church authorities had for some time insisted on appointing Englishmen to the Welsh sees, apparently forgetting —or ignoring—the fact that many of the inhabitants knew little or nothing of the English language and disliked the 'foreigners'.

There is also evidence to show that the failure of the church to uphold what has been called 'standards of moderation, or to maintain an individual clergyman's behaviour appreciably above the social level of the day', had its effect. Bishop Humphreys, who worked in Anglesey shortly before the turn of the 18th century, insisted that before a person was appointed the question should be raised 'is he sober, seemly, moderate in dress . . . does he board in a tavern or ale-house, or does he frequent such houses, except when summoned to visit the sick or to perform some other part of his duty?' The same Bishop declared that meetings of the Anglesey clergy should preferably be held in a church or in a Minister's house—'not in an ale-house if possibly it can be avoided'. He did, however, condescend to add that if ale-house meetings could not be avoided 'then I desire that no ale be drunk in the room of the meetings; and that as soon as business is over, all depart to their respective homes without any sitting to drink'.

At this time the church was the sole authority; its clergy had powers far beyond anything that we understand today. It was the parson who declared which days should be working days and which days should be holidays; it was he who could

D

decide the suitability or otherwise of a man for employment; it was he, who, by his own behaviour and example, could largely determine the character of community life. But neither was the parson's power always exercised with the one objective of getting his flock to church! One entry from William Bulkeley's *Diary* reads for Michaelmas, 1735: 'The Parson proclaimed this was a holy day, but instead of reading service in church he went to Llanfihangell wakes'.

By 1880 or thereabouts more than three-quarters of the population had become non-conformists, and the church in Wales was still bound by the rulings of the Church of England, being the State Church. This rankled, and by 1895 a Parliamentary Bill was brought in for the disestablishment of the Church in Wales. This Bill failed, as did another fourteen years later. After a short time came yet another Bill—this one in 1912—and finally, two years later, the Welsh Church was disestablished.

Another, and very ancient, form of religion in Anglesey was that of the Druids. The Oxford Dictionary defines Druid as 'one of an order of men among the ancient Celts of Gaul and Britain who, according to Caesar, were priests or religious ministers and teachers, but who figure in native Irish and Welsh legend as magicians, sorcerers, soothsayers and the like'.

According to some authorities, Anglesey was second only in importance to Wiltshire as a Druid stronghold. Amid a welter of speculation as to who they were and what they did, Caesar in his description of the customs of Gaul wrote that to these men 'the youth, in great numbers, apply for instruction; they decide in all controversies, public and private; if a crime be committed, if a person be slain, if succession to property, or the boundaries of land be in question—they determine the case, and adjudge the rewards and punishments. If anyone, whether in private or public station refuses to abide by their award, they interdict him from the sacrifices, which is the greatest punishment . . . one Druid who has supreme authority, presides over all the rest, and on his death, if there be one pre-eminent estimation, he succeeds. At a certain season of the year, they hold an assembly in a consecrated place, esteemed the central place of Gaul: hither all who have any controversies repair from every part, and submit to their judgement and decrees.

'The Druids are not accustomed to engage in warfare, nor

do they pay tribute, but are excused from military service, and in every respect are privileged persons. Many become voluntarily attached to them, and others are sent by their parents and relations. The students commit to memory a great number of verses, and some of them continue their study for twenty years . . . their leading principle is that souls do not perish, but pass after death to other bodies; a principle which, in their opinion is the greatest incentive to virtue and contempt of death. They also lecture on the stars and their motion; the magnitude of the earth, and its divisions; on natural history; and on the power and government of God, and instruct the youth in these subjects.'

The Druids were well acquainted with medical botany. They made use of many plants, particularly mistletoe and cowslip, in their rites, and on the 6th of March each year the Chief Druid 'dressed in white, ascended an oak tree and with a consecrated knife, gathered the mistletoe'.

Apart from what Caesar tells us of the customs of the Druids, they made a curious use of verse to put over points of morality. The first line was used as a 'key', the second part was based on some fact of natural history, and the third gave the moral in proverb style. Here are two examples, taken from an 1832 Eisteddfod essay:

Snow of the mountain,
The bird is ravenous for food,
The wind whistles on the head-land,
In distress a relation is the most valuable.

The first day of winter,—severe is the weather,
Unlike the first summer,
None but God can foresee what is to come.

Superstition, mystique, or faith—whatever its basis, Druidism was put down when the Romans came, and it was Mrs. Felicia Hemans, the 19th century poetess, who summed up Anglesey's, and the Druids' feelings about Caesar's men. This is from her poem '*To the Harp*'—

O'er the blue waters with his thousand oars;
Through Mona's oaks he sent the wasting flame;
The Druid shrines lay prostrate on our shores,
He gave their ashes to the wind and sea:
. . . Sing out thou harp, he could not silence thee!

V

GEOLOGY

THE MONA COMPLEX

To the geologist and naturalist, as well as the archaeologist, Anglesey makes a great and unique appeal. Of the mere dozen places in all England and Wales where the old 'floor' underlying later formations of rock can be seen, Anglesey has the most extensive and varied examples. To the ornithologist the island offers a tremendous variety of bird life—residents, many migrants and often rare summer and winter wanderers. The botanist can be happy in the knowledge that from the earliest monastic herbals to the reports of contemporary students, the list of flowering plants has grown to a total of well over 600 identified on this small island.

Among the geologists, perhaps no man has more appreciated the beauty of Anglesey's rocks than Edward Greenly who, in 1895, after spending six years as a member of the staff of the Geological Survey of the Scottish Highlands, started single-handed a detailed survey of the geology of Anglesey, a task which was to take him twenty-four years. In 1919 his memoirs were published—in no small part at his own expense—'by order of the Lords Commissioners of His Majesty's Treasury'. Neither before nor since, has anything so monumental been attempted.

The geological formations of Anglesey are unusually intact. Pre-Cambrian age rocks cover nearly two-thirds of the area and are called the Mona Complex. In it there are nine different main groups of rocks, containing over seventy petrological types and nearly as many rock-forming minerals. Briefly, and with the help of Mr. Greenly's geological memoirs, here is an 'amateur's guide' to some of the rocks found in the nine groups of the Mona Complex:

Holyhead Quartzite: This is probably the most conspicuous on the island. It is white and very uniform in structure. The deeper it is quarried the whiter it seems to become. On Holyhead Mountain, the whole mass (except at the foot of the southern escarpment) is cut through by nearly vertical strips of rock called foliation—the alternation of parallel layers of different minealogical nature.

South Stack Series: These rocks show some of the most striking geological sections in Britain, mainly to be seen laid bare in the tall sea-cliffs. This group, and the Holyhead Quartzite, are the only big sub-divisions of the Mona Complex composed entirely of mechanical sediment. One particularly finely developed rugged tract, although differing slightly geologically, is the Mynydd Mechell.

New Harbour Group: These rocks are so called because there is a fine lot to be seen around the harbour at Holyhead. Geologically in this group come what are called the Green-Mica-Schists, green-coloured layers of crystallised rocks sparkling with little flakes of mica.

Skerries Group: Geologists sub-divide these rocks into the Skerries Grits, the Church Bay Tuffs, and the Tyfry Beds. From these rock formations come many beautifully marked pebbles found on Anglesey beaches. Typical Skerries Grit pebbles are mottled greenish-grey, and the finest are purple.

Gwna Group: The name for this group comes from the little River Gwna, near Bodorgan, being the only district in which all nine sub-divisions of the Mona Complex are found. The formation has a wider distribution than any other in the island, being found at intervals from Carmel Head to Garth Ferry. This group has undergone fewer mineral reconstructions than the rest of the Mona Complex but it has ben excessively broken up. Within the groups are many sub-types, one of which is called the Llanddwyn after the area in which the limestone rock is so well developed. This class of rock varies with great rapidity—often within a yard or two. One type of Llanddwyn rock is a fine, delicate rose colour; another is green; and in many places the rose-green limestones are beautifully studded with green and purple volcanic fragments.

Coedana Granite: There are four main types in this group —normal granite, porphyritic granite, white mica granite and what are called the Fine Veins—but these are rare. Garnet— the deep, blood-red stone used as a gem, is among the minerals found in granite on Anglesey.

The Serpentine-Suite: Mostly dark green but very occasionally red, these rocks are found in winding veins (hence the name serpentine) along either side of the narrow channel between Holyhead and the main part of Anglesey. The rock is usually granular, mottled with a light green colour. At Mynachdy there is a serpentine rich in clusters of minute garnets.

Penmyndd Schists: In this case the rocks are named after a village in the centre of an area of Anglesey in which they abound. The most extensive in this group are the mica-schists, clean and fresh looking quartz rock tinged with pale sea-green. Another type is the glaucophane-schists—unique in Britain.

Apart from the Mona Complex, and taking the same order as used in the Geological Survey, next to be considered are all the rock formations known to be *later* than the Mona Complex.

The area of Baron Hill, Beaumaris, gives its name to a small group which, although later than the Mona Complex, are pre-Ordovician—stepping stones, as it were, across an enormous chronological interval. Nearly all the exposures of these particular rocks, identical in character with the volcanic group of Bangor, are in the Baron Hill Park and in the Llandegfra road.

Of the Ordovician age itself, Anglesey has much to show —in fact, next to those of the Mona Complex these rocks are the most extensive in the island. Their principal area is a large tract of the central and north-western parts of the island in the midst of which is the alluvial tract of Cors-y-Bol. One of the best sections is at Llyn Maelog, near Rhosneigr, where a number of escarpment ridges look down on the lake. All round the coast of Rhosneigr—especially at low tide—excellent sections of overlying shades can be seen. Further north, between Cemaes and Bull Bays, the Ordovician rocks can also be seen, and at Gwfor eight wedges of them are let into the rocks of the earlier Mona Complex.

Silurian Age: At only one place—Parys Mountain--are rocks of Silurian age to be found in Anglesey. The period of these rocks was established by evidence of the kinds of fossils found there.

Upper Palaeozoic: Into this group comes sandstones and limestones. They are well exposed along the coast between Dulas and Lligwy Bays; in the escarpment of Coed-y-gell; and between Mynydd Bodafon and the sea.

Carboniferous Rocks: In extent, this series comes third in importance among Anglesey rock formations. They are of various types—limestones, shale and sandstone included—and the principal area is a five-mile stretch on the east coast running through to Malltraeth Sands. Within the general grouping of carboniferous rocks, the limestones contain coral beds in a few places.

Millstone Grit: On the highest beds of the carboniferous limestone is a sandstone called 'the millstone grit', and some coal measures. The millstone grit can be seen best on the Bodorgan shores. Deep under the sea is coal.

The Red Measures: Bright red-coloured beds, later than the carboniferous rocks, occur at the Malltraeth coal-field and on the side of Menai Strait opposite Caernarvon. The Malltraeth valley beds are the most interesting, being of red sandstone with grey-green marks and soft, blue-grey shades. Pebbles are common in some of the Red Measures, often pitted, dimpled and with a 'polish'.

Drifts and Glaciation: Most of the surface of Anglesey is covered with glacial drift, chiefly boulder clay and some sand and gravel. The blue boulder clay is seen only in deeper sections, but along the eastern margin of the island there is red boulder clay at places from Bull Bay to Beaumaris. The drifts are full of a variety of stones, partly due to the exceptional number of different rocks in the island itself and partly from the pieces of rock which have found their way into Anglesey from other counties surrounding the Irish Sea, as well as from the mountains of Wales itself. Rocks from Caernarvonshire are plentiful all along the shore of the Strait. At Amlwch, and at Holyhead Bay, felsite from somewhere in Lakeland has been identified; granite has come to Anglesey from Galloway; and even small boulders from the Western Isles of Scotland and the Firth of Clyde find their way to Anglesey.

South-westerly winds blow hard, and often, over the island. Along the western seaboard fifteen square miles are covered with blown sand, and at Tywyn Trewan sandy tracts extend two miles inland. Sweeping eastwards the sand has covered much cultivated country, homesteads are buried beneath it and rocks which were grooved and rounded by ice long ago are now being grooved and polished by sand-blast.

A big part of Greenly's studies, naturally enough, were devoted to the Menai Strait, that fifteen miles of river-like channel sometimes as placid as a lake, sometimes moving in a tide-race that can be heard a mile away. Pre-glacial, late-glacial and post-glacial periods all contributed to the formation of the Strait. A strange discovery was made when soundings were taken on the depth of water. On the Anglesey side of the Strait, at Pwllfanogl, the gentle westward slope is suddenly broken by a huge chasm seventy-seven feet deep—about fifty feet below the average level of the Strait floor thereabouts. The hole is thought to have been made in the soft rocks by the cascading force of a waterfall long ago.

The rocks and many of the birds of Anglesey are inseparable. From the end of March and early April the steep ledges of the cliffs all around the island are increasingly populated by thousands of visitors—guillemots, razorbills, and that quite delightful little bird, the puffin. By the middle of April the first advanced parties of tern, or sea swallows, can be seen in the Menai Strait, and by early May, the tern will have spread all along the coast forming colonies on every suitable islet or rocky outcrop—for instance, at Rhosneigr, Llanddwyn Island, Rhoscolyn (an official bird sanctuary) and on the Skerries.

From the manner of the flight of tern it is easy to see why they are called sea swallows—and these birds are courageous as well as graceful. At Rhosneigr, for instance, and just a short distance off-shore is a group of rocks rising out of the sea and accessible on foot at low tide, called, as a group, Starvation Island. Here many hundred of common tern, arctic tern, and a few of the less prolific types such as the roseate tern, each year raise their families. The terns resent a human invader. They swoop, swirl and fly down upon him sometimes in a mass attack, sometimes just in pairs. In the nesting season in these tern colonies I have found it difficult to walk through the grass beyond the high tide mark on top of the rocks without crushing eggs or chicks in a tern's nest.

A 'playful' bird common in Anglesey is the Oyster Catcher. These noisy, nervous and active sea-birds are, of course, common enough; but their devilment is a delight to watch. They will be particularly happy if they can torment a dog over miles of shore rocks, flying very slowly and very near to ground level pretending to let the dog catch them. The dog never does, of course, but the game can go to point of exhaustion on a dog's part, or until the oyster catchers break off and indulge in one of their 'piping' parties. The piping of oyster catchers, the translucent green of the flat, slab-like rocks at low tide and, on clear evenings, the sun setting over the Irish Sea are delights to be heard and seen at many places on the west coast of Anglesey.

On the north coast is Cemlyn Bay and a nearby bird sanctuary which, in mid-winter, is populated with hundreds of duck. Here I have seen shovelers, teal, pochards, and red shank. Go inland, in a south-easterly direction, and near the village of Carreglefn, you will find a small inland lake—a lonely spot favoured by big groups of black-headed gulls, mallard, tufted duck, and moorhen.

Two classic places for the bird watcher on Anglesey are, naturally enough, the South Stack cliffs at Holyhead—where the peregrine falcon can be seen, and Llanddwyn island—a tiny tag-end of land pointing out like a finger over the sand-swept Newborough Warren, due west across the Menai Strait from Caernarvon. Llanddwyn is an intriguing, mystical place reached from Newborough over a mile or so of sand dunes rich in wild flowers. On the Warren itself there are also great blocks of coniferous trees planted by the Forestry Commission since, in 1940, they took over 2,000 or more acres of this wild expanse. On a walk to this 'island' with its little ruined church, lighthouse and a few cottages, I saw such birds as the wood wren and willow wren, all the tit family, finches, the wheater and nightjar.

Westward of Llanddwyn and rising out of the sea is a large rock called Bird Island. Here operates some sort of bird law of racial purity for the tern species; entry by any other bird causes trouble. Let any wandering gull or other bird attempt to land here and he will soon suffer fierce 'dive-bombing' from the tern attackers. Even the sight of a big ship is enough to put into the air every single bird on this rock—and there must be many, many hundreds of them. The noise is terrific since the tern, even individually, is an exceptionally noisy creature. They have a number of cries, but the commonest of them is a shrill scream and this, from the colony as a whole, goes on intermittently from dawn till dusk.

On Llanddwyn it is easy to share the emotions of Maclair Boraston, a naturalist who 'did' Anglesey on a bicycle in the early days of this century and who wrote in the language of the time : 'If one should stay long at Llanddwyn the passive spirit of the place would drug the mind, lulling all human hopes and fears into acquiescence, given that one great condition, to hear the soft lapping of the water in the coves, stealing the land by grains.

If, sooner or later, all must go, why struggle, why resist? Let it go, one would say, so let it go easily, part of the everlasting interchange of land and sea. When, in the winter nights, the wind once whipped the gravel from the beach and sent the big seas pounding up the cove, so the ground trembles to hear the pounding surf rise in revolt. This one would fain have at it, and curb it, and dam it off with dykes and stones and iron, and let it gnash its teeth on them and break them.' Incidentally, the writer of this piece left Llanddwyn with his bicycle strapped on to the side of a household donkey, which was the normal means of carrying freight over the sand warren beyond!

The peninsula of Llanddwyn is not much more than half a mile long and less than a quarter wide. In the centre is a small valley carpeted, when I first saw it, with the wild rose spreading low on sandy soil. Benedictine monks once made this lonely place their retreat, and a cross which centuries later was put up to commemorate their earlier occupation has inscribed on it these words in Welsh and English:

They lie around; did living tread
This sacred ground; now silent, dead.

A larger cross on the headland itself is inscribed with the word Dwynwen, the name of the daughter of Brychan, who in the 5th century founded a monastery hereabouts. Dwynwen, herself a solitary virgin, founded a religious house and, according to one earlier chronicler, became the guardian saint of lovers and the Welsh equivalent to St. Valentine. After she was buried here, Dwynwen's tomb became a shrine where lights were burned continually. Old legend has it that, innocent maid though she was, Dwynwen drew all lovers to her. She also seems to have helped the Llanddwyn monks to thrive financially, so much so that they built an abbey with their riches—eventually obliterated by the sea, or sand.

Incidentally, the income of former Rectors of Llanddwyn was derived from the offerings of pilgrims to the shrine of St. Dwynwen, and the living was one of the richest in the Diocese of Bangor.

The last rector of Llanddwyn as an independent parish was Richard Kyffin, later Dean of Bangor, who died in 1502. He had a house on the island where he 'carried on his crafty intrigues against Richard III'. Llanddwyn was reputed to be the centre of the plot which culminated in the Battle of Bosworth in 1485 and the seizure of the throne by Henry Tudor, of Anglesey origin.

Each year there is a service in the ruined church of St. Dwynwen, attended mostly by the parishioners of Newborough who go to protest against the restriction of island rights of access which the public appear to have enjoyed for at least five centuries—but probably much longer. In 1965 the pilgrimage was led by the Bishop of Bangor and encouragement to the pilgrims, who marched in defiance of the Keep Off notices put up during the year by the Nature Conservancy, came from the Rector of Newborough, the Rev. John Parry.

First, it was the Royal Society for the Protection of Birds who used locks and chains to close part of the island to the public but the Society's interests have since been absorbed by the Nature Conservancy—some of whose wardens have been described as being a little over-zealous in carrying out their duties and so provoking hostility among the local people. The Forestry Commission, too, have to face their share of the criticism.

As far back as 1948 the then Lord Newborough, who had leased the island to the Royal Society for the Protection of Birds as a bird sanctuary, stated that he thought that so long as the public did not harm or disturb the birds, and provided people kept to the paths, there was not the slightest reason why they should not go there. But this is not everyone's point of view.

The whole forest area of Newborough which, amalgamated with Pentraeth, and called Môn Forest, consists of blown sand merging in places into marsh. Of the trees planted by the Forestry Commission, Corsican Pine is the most numerous. Scots Pine has proved unable to stand up to the sea wind well enough to yield good timber, but it is used for interplanting and supplying thatching material. Sitka Spruce is successful up to a point, mainly being found on the marshes, and the Commission has planted some White Spruce in parts of the forest. Pinus Contorta grows vigorously on the winter lakes when these can be drained.

The bigger and higher sand dunes are constantly moving and partly disintegrating in the high winds. On these dunes there is little else but deep-rooted marram grass, with dwarf willow in the winter lakes. The Commission has had a big problem in preventing 'dust bowl' conditions in the area by various methods of 'fixing' the sand dunes, either by planting a cover of seeding grass, weeds and marram or by thatching the dunes. A great deal of work has been done recently to increase and improve forest roads, both to facilitate timber extractions and to provide better access for the lorries carting the brash for thatching—about twelve lorry loads are needed for every acre, and about fifty acres a year is 'fixed' in this way from being blown away.

There are two small trees nurseries in Môn Forest which have proved of great value because Anglesey's climate permits work to go on there when all other nurseries are held up by wet, frost or snow. The trees grown include Maritime Pine, Pinus Radiata, Cupressus Maerscarpa and Pinus Ponderosa *var.* Jeffreyi. No shrubs have proved of much use, either for stabilising the sand or for growing to provide thatching material.

When criticism is made of restrictions to public freedom— to say nothing of the protests from some quarters about Commission plantings being 'regimented blocks of dark trees foreign to the natural landscape' and all that, it is worth pondering the fact that Newborough is more than a timber producing forest (about 5,000 tons a year is the target); it is there primarily to stabilise a desert of shifting sand, to use what was formerly little more than a wilderness and to give permanent employment to local men in an area where work is not always easy to find.

The forest is of considerable biological interest, and the area south of Môn Forest has been made a National Nature Reserve.

Here, and all over the island of Anglesey, botanists have been talking about treasures they have found since at least the 17th century, and indeed one of the most historic botanical tours was made in 1639 by Thomas Johnson, a herbalist from London, and two friends—Paul Sone and Edward Morgan. In 1641 Johnson wrote—in Latin—an account of this visit in *The Botanic Mercury.* He describes finding—as we do to-day on the rocks of Anglesey—such plants as Sea Lavender, Rock Samphire, Glasswort, Sea Purslane and the Sea Aster. Among the sandhills is a wild pansy, *Viola curtisii Forst,* Tufted Centaury and Sea Spurge.

In 1726 Samuel Brewer (1670-1742), born at Trowbridge, and Dillenius, the first Sherardian professor of botany at Oxford, spent six days in Anglesey and among the plants they found and recorded for the first time in Britain were the Bristley Ox-tongue (*Picris Echioides*); the Grass of Parnassus (*Parnassia palustris L.*); a rare Hawkweed (*Hieracium acutus*); and Pond-weed (*Potamogeton niten Weber*). Three plants on the island at this time were used by the women for colour dyes—yellow from Euphorbia *paralias,* black from the Burnet Rose and red from lichen.

Throughout the later half of the 19th century there was great activity in systematic botany throughout Britain, and it became fashionable to compile local lists and to secure new county records. Thus Johns E. Griffith in his *Flora of Anglesey and Caernarvonshire* 1894, mentioned in particular the 'unusual varieties of Ragwort found on Holy Island', and other writers listed plants found on Puffin Island as including Buck's Horn Plaintain (*Plantago coronopus*); Scurvy Grass (*Cochlearia officinalis*); Rock Samphire; and Iris *foetidissima.*

A never ending source of delight for visitors to Anglesey is the flowering together of blue Harebells and pink Thrift along rocky parts of the coast; the great abundance of Foxgloves, Rock Roses and Columbines; and, in secluded leafy lanes if you search diligently, the exquisite yellow variety of wild rose.

VI

SHIPPING

SOVEREIGNS IN THE SAND

While watching waves glistening round
   Maltreath alone,
In silent grief listening to sea-birds hollow
   moan,
I wish I was sleeping in the dark heaving
   tide,
Whose solemn depths are keeping my darling
   dead bride.
                              —*Old Welsh Song.*

Stories of shipwreck off the coasts of Anglesey and North Wales are many, but two major tragedies stand out never to be forgotten.

Early in the 19th century steam vessels had already replaced sailing ships in the maintenance of a considerable traffic along the Anglesey coast. The first steamship out of Holyhead for Ireland sailed in 1816; a steam packet, the Cambria, connected North Wales with Liverpool in 1821; and in the following year the first steamer sailed on a regular service from Menai Strait to Liverpool—she was called The Albion and was like a number of other ships plying the coastwise trade, a paddle steamer something between 150-200 tons with engines of only about 70 h.p., but rigged for sail as well.

Not many years after the opening of the passenger service a steamship called the Rothsay Castle was put into use during the winter season of 1830-31 and this vessel was to become an historic, if tragic, name in sea annals. On her first appearance she was commanded by 'D. Davies, Master', but when regular sailings began in 1831 she was commanded by an officer of the Royal Navy, one Lieut. Atkins. Whatever we subsequently read, or think, about Lieut. Atkins' command of a ship, one fact should be remembered that the Rothsay Castle had, in fact, been built in the very earliest days of steam navigation, on the Clyde in 1816. Probably the idea then was that she should have done nothing much more than sail 'doon the watter' of the Firth of Clyde. A local shipowner, Mr. Edward Watson, bought her in 1830, and after first contemplating using her on the run between Glasgow and Ireland, finally decided to put her into service between Anglesey and Liverpool. Whether or not this vessel was ever fit for safe passenger service now seems doubtful.

The tragedy which eventually befell the Rothsay Castle is a sorry comment on the earlier boasts of her new owner who had advertised this vessel on her run out of Anglesey as being 'superbly fitted up for the accommodation and comfort of passengers and, from her easy draught of water enabling her to go close inshore, ensuring a smooth passage and an opportunity of viewing the beautiful scenery along the Welsh coast'.

Under the command of Lieut. Atkins, the Rothsay Castle left Liverpool with the last of a morning ebb tide at noon on August 17, 1831. This was two hours after Lieut. Atkins' scheduled time of departure. He had delayed because of 'a large number of passengers seeking tickets' and because of the rather longwinded business of loading a coach on board. By the time Lieut. Atkins sailed there were about 100 passengers, most of them parties from Lancashire towns.

The night before there had been a severe gale. Even that very morning an American ship tried to leave the river at Liverpool but was forced to return. However, despite a heavy swell and a stiff north-westerly breeze, the Rothsay Castle sailed out. But before the vessel was out of the river the tide had already turned and the wind was freshening.

By the time this ship was fifteen miles out of Liverpool those few passengers who were not already prostrate with seasickness knew there was trouble; the captain knew that he was not only off course but way behind his time schedule. Even a passing ship—The Prince Llewellyn bound for Liverpool from Anglesey —noticed with astonishment the Rothsay's course. Account has it that the only man aboard the Rothsay who did not seem to be either ill or worried was the captain himself. At three o'clock in the afternoon he ate and drank well in his cabin. He remained below for two hours while his ship laboured along the Welsh coast. While the captain's port still flowed liberally enough, the sea too was flowing freely—through the axles of the paddles.

Firemen found it hard to maintain fires. Progress became slower and slower.

The passengers begged Lieut. Atkins to return to Liverpool, but he refused. Relevant or not, accounts of this tragedy report the reputation of Lieut. Atkins as being that of a good officer who 'seems to have indulged to excess in alcohol to the prejudice of his manners and judgment'. The storm was getting worse and the night closing in, but the captain made no signals to passing vessels. By eight o'clock that evening the Rothsay was abreast of the Little Orme and from that point it took no less than two more hours to reach the Great Orme!

From this point the ship had to steam into the teeth of the storm if she was to make at all the safe channel between Puffin Island and the Dutchman's Bank leading to Beaumaris. The ladies' cabin was awash, the deck crowded with the seasick, and the captain himself 'offending the ladies with his language when they appealed to his gallantry'. The night was black, without either moon or stars, and the Rothsay's engines spluttered and stopped. The wind was driving the ship back to the southward, and—beam on—she hit the coast so hard that the old accounts speak of the shock 'electrifying those who were suffering from seasickness'.

For the first time Lieut. Atkins became aware of his difficulties. He ordered the jib to be hoisted with the hope of bringing the ship's head round to the south-east—but that was about all he did do, for everyone seems to have been left to their own devices. One passenger appears to have suggested at least the showing of a light and the discharge of a gun as some sign of their distress; neither the captain or his officers showed any interest in the idea and no help came. Next, the funnel of the Rothsay Castle collapsed and soon after that the paddle boxes, which had become a refuge for some of the passengers, broke away and it was 'every man for himself'. Perhaps typical of his curious behaviour throughout the ill-fated voyage, it is reported that about this hour Lieut. Atkins informed his passengers that the ship was quite safe and that they were on the point of arrival in Beaumaris. Perhaps he was doing it with the best of intensions of lessening the horror for all concerned, but by two o'clock in the morning the Rothsay Castle had completely broken up. Even before the end, nearly all her passengers had been swept off and drowned—if they had not earlier been killed

64

Puffin Island is now uninhabited, the home only of sea birds and rabbits.

Relics of a civilisation of long ago. Part of a chambered tomb or cromlech, near Rhoscolyn.

by falling rigging and timbers. The death roll was ninety-nine out of 120 on board. And yet in nearby Beaumaris no-one had the slightest idea what was happening.

May be it is cruel, but the old proverb 'it is an ill wind . . .' does seem pathetically true. During the following few weeks after the tragedy of the Rothsay Castle, Beaumaris boomed. They cancelled the Strait regatta as a gesture, but the hotels were full. Money and drink flowed. In their hundreds they came to gape at the remains of a ship on the Dutchman's Bank. Sadly enough the same ghoulish kind of behaviour was to repeat itself on another point of the Anglesey coast twenty-five years later, at the village of Moelfre. This was the scene in October 1859 of the sinking of the treasure ship, Royal Charter, an iron-built auxiliary steam clipper of 2,719 tons and one of the finest vessels in the Liverpool and Australian Navigation Company's fleet.

The date was October 26 when the ill-fated Royal Charter—returning from the Australian gold rush with over £3,000,000 worth of bullion and valuables—was pounded to pieces off Point Lynas in one of the most dramatic shipping disasters ever to take place around the entire British coasts. Out of a total of 472 passengers only eighteen of the crew and twenty passengers lived. Every woman and child aboard perished.

In full view of the Welsh villagers assembled on the rocks only a few yards from where the Royal Charter split in two, these people died, most of them with their pockets and money belts bulging with gold. None of the victims was drowned—every one had been battered to death on the rocks, including a boy seaman who had travelled 16,000 miles only to perish, seen by his father, half a mile from his home. Those who were not battered to death, the handful of bruised and mutilated survivors, owed their lives to strange flukes of the sea which flung them not on to the rocks but to the beach within reach of the Anglesey villagers. Not only was there death everywhere, there was gold everywhere. And it wasn't long before ugly things began to happen.

The Royal Charter was many miles off course and the weather atrocious. Apparently, some 300 miles of country was swept by a cyclonic type of storm, moving north and blowing gusts of 100 miles an hour in an anti-clockwise direction. The damage to shipping, railways, and other transport

65

was colossal. The breakwater at Holyhead was smashed; the railway track through to Chester broken in two places, and in the Menai Strait itself forty coastal ships lay crippled. The toll round our coasts of this one storm, including the loss of the Royal Charter, was 133 shipwrecks and 800 lives lost.

'It was a calm, hazy autumn day when the Royal Charter steamed past Holyhead at about 5.00 p.m. on October 25', wrote a correspondent in *The Times*. 'Five hours later the weather had become so bad the ship was soon in trouble . . . each gust of wind breaking down upon the ship with a blow like a hammer, testing everything in the way of masts and rigging to its utmost . . . from that time to between 2.00 and 3.00 p.m. the battle increased in volume . . . the darkness was inpenetrable, while the hoarse roar of the wind drowned every other sound save the dull booming waves upon the rocks'.

By 10.30 p.m. the Royal Charter had drifted into a position east of Point Lynas. The only practical course for her Master, Captain Taylor, was to let go the anchors. With every gust the strain on the anchor cables increased. At 1.30 a.m. on October 26th, the port cable parted at the hawser hold; and an hour later the starboard cable went too. The Royal Charter drifted helplessly towards the shore. Sometime after three o'clock in the morning she hit the sand, stern first. The passengers were up and dressed and assembled in the saloon and all, said the captain, would be safely ashore come daylight. His confidence was short-lived. Ninety minutes later the port quarter of the Royal Charter was broken on the shelving rocks and water came rushing in through the ship's broken sky lights—all this in total darkness. Shortly after seven, just as the Chief Officer entered the saloon to call the first party forward for rescue, the Royal Charter parted amidships and, within minutes, was engulfed by the sea.

Nearby beaches and rocks were soon littered with wreckage and mutilated bodies. Soon the same gold fever which had earlier drawn these men to Australia in turn drew men and women to the coves around Moelfre. The villagers knew only too well, through observing where driftwood normally fetched up, where to look for the spoil. Not only were the passengers carrying a great wealth back from Australia, but the ship itself had on board a great amount of valuables. One passenger alone was said to have carried a fortune (in those days) of £10,000;

another, a bookmaker, who absconded with his Australian clients' money, £4,000. The villagers in some cases carried back literally buckets full of gold to nearby cottages. It was not uncommon for one man to pick up a hundred or more gold sovereigns from the dead.

Soon after the disaster official salvage operations were started and the local inhabitants of Moelfre were recruited by the Crown to help retrieve some of the lost property. Salvage tugs and divers were also soon on the scene and nearly all of the consigned bullion was retrieved. Nevertheless, anything up to half a million pounds worth of gold belonging to the individual passengers was 'floating about'. Some was, without doubt, stolen; and some—who knows how much—buried in the sand. Despite the fact that salvage operations went on for no fewer than fourteen years, and many hundreds of sovereigns were found among the twisted iron-work of the Royal Charter, there may well be, even to this day, some gold somewhere in these sands. With a bucket and spade and the exciting story of the famous golden shipwreck, could any child ask for a better incentive to dig and keep digging?

Not only children on holiday, but all sorts of people have since been trying to find the buried treasure off the Anglesey coast, including a party of spare-time divers from Nottinghamshire. Several of the men, members of an underwater swimming club, are miners and one of them, when the search was planned, said he and his team-mates believed the value of the gold on the sea bed was £30,000 or more 'and we mean to probe until we find it'.

But, however much there is, the gold is still there!

Four months after the Royal Charter disaster the wreck was sold to the original ship owners for £1,000. Even *The Daily Telegraph* correspondent, who had earlier got so worked up about local 'thieves', was able to report that 'to the credit of the Anglesey peasantry the survivors spoke with gratitude of the hearty generosity manifested by the people. They saved many lives, took them into their homes, put them into warm beds and gave them the best they could afford . . .' The dead of the Royal Charter, who came back with their riches, lie buried without them in a grave on Anglesey where 'so many are so strangely brought together'.

These tragedies of the Rothsay Castle and the Royal Charter

are grimly factual—but the island also has its share of lighter sea legends.

South-eastwards from Rhos-y-gader Farm, near Trearddur Bay, is a large cave. In a house near here there lived Dick-bach and his wife Betsy-mawr, whose son had years before run away to sea. Dick-bach and Betsy-mawr were experts in gathering profitable wreckage whenever it was washed ashore, and 'if the hunting was good' (as they used to say) this couple would hide their loot in the cave—both out of reach of the tide and safe from prying eyes—until they could conveniently dispose of their profits. Betsy was apparently very fat. She needed both hands for clambering among the rocks of the cave and therefore hit on the idea of wearing an enormous pair of blue woollen breeches which served to carry whatever cargo the couple found.

One winter's night when a ship was wrecked off this coast several cases of whisky were washed up on the shore. Not only Dick and Betsy but most of the other locals turned out—ostensibly to help the Customs officials in their salvage work. Soon a number of inhabitants are said to have been lying drunken and incapable on the beach, and the good Dick-bach went the rounds pouring salt water into their mouths to (as he explained afterwards) 'put the flames out'. While Dick was busy on his mercy mission, Betsy was loading up her breches with six bottles of whisky each side. So weighed down, she started waddling along the beach towards her famous cave, but the clinking of the bottles aroused the suspicions of the Customs officials one of whom, it is said, sternly asked Betsy 'What have you got there?'

Betsy's simple retort was 'Mind your own business—and search me *if* you dare'. All this went on in front of a grinning crowd of onlookers and apparently the Customs man decided that the least embarrassing thing would be to let Betsy go her way. She made the cave all right, but later when Dick—himself none too sober by then—arrived, he found poor Betsy in a huddled heap on the slippery boulders of the cave, hopelessly drunk. Beyond Betsy lay the lifeless body of the seafaring son they had not seen for so long. He had been washed into the cave from his ship.

At another part of the Anglesey coast, in a corner of Penrhos Bay, are the words *Tyger, September 17, 1819* engraved on a stone about two feet high and facing the sea over the Black Arch. They commemorate the remarkable story of a dog's devotion in saving the lives of a sea captain, two other men and a boy, from a sinking ship.

The story runs that a ketch bound for Liverpool struck a rock during thick fog, and in a very few minutes, sank in deep water. The ship's captain had only the vaguest idea of his whereabouts but his big Retriever dog called Tyger sensed in which direction the land lay—that dogs can undoubtedly do this is believed to be due to their acute sense of hearing, enabling them to detect an echo from the cliffs caused by their own barking.

Whether that is so or not, this dog started swimming strongly from the sinking ship. The captain and others of the crew decided to follow Tyger. Only the captain was a strong swimmer and he helped his two men in turn while the boy managed to grasp and hold on to the dog's collar. By the time they eventually sighted the cliffs through the fog they were so exhausted that had it not been for the courage of the dog it is doubtful whether any of them should have landed at all. Tyger, it is said, having brought the boy within reach of the rocks, turned back and swam to the captain but, because of one of the other men was in a much worse plight, the captain sent Tyger to the man's aid. Remarkable though it seems, the dog apparently seized the man's clothes and again succeeded in reaching the shore. Nor was this the end, for again Tyger swam out to sea and gave the last ounce of his strength in enabling both his master and the other seaman to reach the rocks. That done, the dog collapsed, feebly licking the hand of his master, and died.

VII

INDUSTRY

THE ANGLESEY FARM

The people of Anglesey are Welsh by birth, islanders by environment, farmers and farm workers by necessity—even though modern industries and the tourist trade are constantly providing new types of employment. Of the island's 152,000 acres, about forty-six per cent is in holdings between twenty and one hundred acres. These small farms are worked by full-time farmers and making a satisfactory living presents a big problem.

The response to the government's Small Farm Scheme, introduced in 1959 to provide grants towards agricultural improvements, indicates Anglesey's needs. Through the Scheme over £500,000 has been paid to the island's small farmers.

Agricultural Return Statistics 1965

Size of Farms	No. of Farms	Crops and Grass Acres held by various Groups	% Land in each Group
Farms 1—19¾ acres	1,649	17,000 (approx.)	12%
Farms 20—99¾ acres	1,249	61,000 (approx.)	46%
Farms 100—150 acres	174 ⎫	57,000 (approx.)	42%
Farms 150 and over	164 ⎭		

As in other parts of the country, developments in agricultural mechanisation and cropping techniques are encouraging the amalgamation of uneconomic small farms, a process which has been going on ever since the war. There are in Anglesey today about 1,000 fewer holdings than in 1939. Amalgamation is thus taking place fairly rapidly—but unfortunately not in a very orderly pattern.

The advantages enjoyed by the Anglesey farmer are the inherent fertility of the soil and a mild climate. The neighbouring county of Caernarvonshire is more than double the size of Anglesey yet there are more acres of crops and grass in Anglesey. There are roughly eight acres of good land for every acre of rough grazing in Anglesey, as compared with one acre + rough grazing for every acre of crops and grass in Caernarvonshire. Any system of farming, be it dairying, beef production, fat lamb production, arable farming, early potatoes, can be adopted profitably. The Anglesey farmer has many alternatives to choose from, whereas the mountain farmers of Wales are restricted to keeping ewes and single suckling cows.

Anglesey is a finishing county—every agricultural product can be produced and finished for consumption off the farm. It also finishes cattle and sheep from the hill counties. Again the finished products must be exported to other parts of the country for consumption, for example seven gallons of milk out of every eight goes to the consuming centres.

The fertile land enabled the county not only to earn its title as the Granary of Wales, but also to produce crops yielding well above the national average. Barley and oats are the traditional crops, and up to two tons to the acre are obtained on the well-drained soils. Spring wheat is also a good crop, with similar yields. At today's values grain crops are worth over £300,000 a year to Anglesey farmers, although of this the quantity actually sold off the farm amounts to about £100,000.

Whatever other factors have governed the fortunes and misfortunes of Anglesey farming, its efforts—like others—came into prominence during the war. The 1914-18 war produced its burst of agricultural drive, of big cropping programmes, of land reclamation. But it did not last. Within a relatively short space of time after that war prices and production had dropped and the farms again sunk into inertia—until the next war came in 1939. But wars apart, there was a 'disciple' to come on the scene after the first World War—Sir George Stapledon, pioneer of grassland technique and the first Director of the famous Welsh Plant Breeding Station formed in 1919. The results of this man's work has been the improvement of grass not merely in this country but over a large part of the world, enabling a big increase in stock to be carried on our farms. He it was who interpreted in practical terms the truth that few achievements are of greater value to mankind than 'making two blades of grass grow where one, or none, grew before'. Neither does it end with better grass and, therefore, more stock. The extra number of animals add more to the manurial treatment of the land, so that subsequently it can be ploughed and grow heavier crops of grain.

Between 1939 and 1945 there were wartime agricultural committees able to enforce the late Sir George's teachings and few areas of the United Kingdom benefited more than Wales and, with it, Anglesey. Almost overnight, the neglect of years was wiped out; derelict acres, both in the areas of low-lying land and in the hills, were brought back into cultivation and the county's total output of farm produce was put up considerably. This increase was again helped forward when, in 1954, heavily infested areas were largely cleared of rabbits by the spread of the virus disease myxomatosis.

Gradually, from being such a famous cropping and beet area, Anglesey began to put the emphasis on milk production— a process undoubtedly stimulated by the setting up, in 1944, of the Milk Marketing Board—and the security it offered of a monthly cheque to milk producers. Previously most milk on the land was made into butter and was sold wholesale to shops or retail to customers in towns; and in the remoter parts the butter was sold in unsalted lumps to dealers—for whatever price the dealer could get. After an MMB collecting centre was opened at Llangefni in 1945, production of milk in Anglesey rose from 1,750,000 gallons to over 5,000,000 gallons a year in six years. Today, the milk output in Anglesey is running at nearly 8,000,000 gallons.

The following figures show quite clearly that nowadays stock, not arable farming, is the expanding industry in Anglesey, and total numbers have increased heavily since 1939, despite a loss of over 6,000 acres of farm land during that time to housing and roads.

Type of Stock	1939	1952	1965	1966
Cattle:				
Dairy Cows	14,463	19,150	18,189	18,242
Other Cattle	35,598	34,970	52,510	53,453
Total Cattle	50,061	54,120	70,699	71,695
Milk Production (Gallons)	1,086,000	6,479,000	8,138,000	7,871,000
Pigs:	10,561	16,000	18,396	15,642
Sheep:				
Breeding Ewes	90,396	58,759	101,176	104,024
Total Sheep	179,059	137,262	205,557	212,060

Numerically, there are on Anglesey—as in other parts of the Principality—more sheep than any other livestock, and a tremendously valuable crop it is to the Anglesey farmer. The lamb crop alone is worth nearly £750,000. The island became the foster home of the Wiltshire breed because of its ability, when crossed with Welsh sheep, to produce early fat lambs, and breeders from Anglesey now dominate world shows.

In common with farmers elsewhere, Anglesey sheep men are troubled with the problem disease called live fluke—in one particular bad year sheep deaths on the island exceeded 15,000 from this scourge alone. The answer lies in better land drainage, to keep the animals' feet out of waterlogged grass, and stricter measures to control the secondary larvae carrying host, a small snail. Yet another problem for the Anglesey farm—and one which is growing in proportion to the spread of imported industry—is manpower. The smaller holdings get along well enough with family labour but the drift of men from the bigger farms is causing hardship.

Although agricultural output is going up, the labour force on Anglesey farms is now half what it was in 1952 and manpower is becoming a scarce product. There are not much more than 1,000 full-time employees, and the island's farms are largely run by family labour—with most farmers of today themselves farmers' sons.

An investigation made in 1925 into the social origin of Welsh farmers showed that out of 800 cases surveyed, less than a quarter had been able to move up the ladder from being farm workers to becoming farmers. Apart from the cash difficulties, few farm workers stayed on to become farmers because of a shortage of cottages. Often those cottages which did become empty were in too bad a state to live in, and it is easy to see why life even down a coal mine became more attractive than life on the land.

From various sources, usually note-books kept by farmers in the past, we can get some idea of wage rates and conditions. A century ago nearly all the farm workers lived in at the farm, paying something for their board and lodging. An adult man got seven shillings for the week's work. This became eighteen shillings by 1914; £1 13s. 0d. by 1939; and a basic £11 11s. 0d. at the time this book was written.

By the beginning of the 18th century landlords had taken over the bulk of Wales and Anglesey. They were divorced from the farmer in outlook and language because most of them were absentee landlords. They treated the countryside as little more than a way of earning cash and their outlook politically, socially and domestically was based on the idea that gentlemen lived and played in London; estates and farms were all very well for sport—but only the vulgar *lived* there.

A turning point might, however, have come about the middle of the same century when the great agriculturalist Arthur Young visited Wales, and the work of such other prominent people such as Coke of Norfolk was beginning to spread to the remoter parts of the U.K. The better land-owners tried to introduce the more scientific processes, but more often than not they failed—partly through the reluctance of 'traditional' farmers to see that it was in their best interests to move with the times. With the exception of a temporary lull during the French wars, agriculture in the island went down and down. By the early 19th century it was slump in the full sense of the word, with farms being sold for anything the place would fetch and the labour force on the poverty line.

Politics caused trouble because even if the ballot was secret, the landlord was, in fact, nearly always tipped off whenever a tenant was known to be voting against the Tory policy the landlords stood for. There was one short answer by the landlords in those days—the farmers were merely turned out of their homes and land, whether their families had been there hundreds of years or not. No wonder that, when they could, the displaced farmers voted for Liberal reform.

As far as crops are concerned, the mild climate of Anglesey has a profound effect on production. Temperatures are not dissimilar to those in Cornwall and, as in that county, even horticultural bulbs have been grown commercially. Indeed, experiments on this score have been made for many years. Back in 1908 an Anglesey Bulb Growers' Association was formed. Headquarters were at Llanfair P.G., and a profitable business grew up, particularly in growing narcissus, tulip and lily bulbs, and in a very short time the company thrived so well that they were able to declare a dividend of ten per cent on the original shares. Despite this initial enterprise, plus suitable soils and climate, bulb growing never became for the island the profitable thing it is in Cornwall or, more so, in Lincolnshire, where today more daffodils are grown than in Holland itself. Another crop tried in Anglesey, but without commercial success, was tobacco.

Much more important is fruit growing, but here again, despite the right climate conditions, such as those enjoyed in the West Country where fruit is a crop, it has never caught on in Anglesey largely, perhaps, because of the high winds and lack of shelter belts. (Several hundred years ago it was observed that the remote inhabitants of Wales 'have neither orchards nor gardens, but gladly eat the fruits of both when given to them!'). Be that as it may, farming—real farming—always was, and is now, Anglesey's main occupation.

True enough, there is no honour for a prophet in his own land. Still less for a prophet from outside—even so, and with or without a crystall ball, one cannot avoid trying to find the answer to the question 'where does the Anglesey farmer go from here?' The prosperity of an island like this, with a big potential as a holiday area, must be linked with its basic all-the-year round industry—agriculture. There are opportunities for developing farming, not by climbing on an over-loaded band wagon, but by building a band wagon of their own, and taking it to the end point of food distribution—the table in home, in hotel and guest-house. A menu of imported frozen lamb, with Italian cauliflower, Dutch potatoes, Swedish tinned peas and a chemically preserved mint sauce from the East End is not Anglesey fare. Neither is crab from Japan, or canned strawberries from the States.

The land of Anglesey can, and should, provide in sufficient and well-marketed quantities a 'full board'. Lamb, in quality and quantity to suit the market; young beef; bacon and pork produced from skim milk and island-grown barley; and early potatoes sold under a brand name, followed by enough main crop for the island's homes, factories and schools throughout the year; and enough grain crops to supplement the grass diet of dairy cattle, to feed beef and still leave some for export.

This way, not only would the future of this great industry be assured. Its efforts would be reflected, and a still greater prosperity enjoyed, by the tourist trade.

VIII

THE RETURN TO WORK

Isaac, a fine youth from the South,
Like unto the flow of the sea were his
    manners,
Of modesty and gentleness,
And elegant mead-drinking;
Where he buries his weapon
Retaliation can be forgotten.
He saw not the cruel as uncruel nor the
    sure as uncertain.
His swordstroke rang through the heads of
    mothers.
A bulwark in battle, praiseworthy was he,
    son of Gwydneu.

Aneirin (6th century)
y Gododdin
translated from the Welsh by
D. M. Lloyd.

Agriculture and tourism bring nearly £10,000,000 a year into Anglesey, and are far and away the island's biggest industries, providing work for the majority of Anglesey's inhabitants. For many generations these industries were, apart from mining and quarrying, almost the only sources of employment since—through the lack of economic investment in industry—Anglesey did not share in Britain's industrial revolution.

The population reached its peak in the mid-19th century when so many Irishmen and others found jobs in the building of road and rail communications, of Holyhead harbour and in the then thriving copper mining at Parys Mountain, near Amlwch. By the beginning of this century people were leaving Anglesey; major construction work of bridges, roads and railways was complete, the copper mines were closed by competition from cheaper producers in Chile and elsewhere overseas, and the income from family farms was insufficient—so that by 1939 the population of Anglesey was down to only 46,000, the lowest in a century. During the thirties, of those that remained two out of every five men had no work, and this figure did not include unemployed farm workers.

The wartime need for all-out food production had, as elsewhere, an entirely beneficial effect on Anglesey farming and with the improvement of essential services such as electricity, gas and piped water the first steps were taken to lift the island out of its economic depression. Since the last war about 10,000 people have been added to Anglesey's population; over twenty new factories have opened, others are expanding; the world's largest nuclear power station is at Wylfa; and unemployment was halved in a period of less than five years. To help the island make such an impressive come back, 300 miles of new water mains were laid, over 100 miles of road improvements and re-surfacing were completed in five years and twelve new bridges built.

Dominating the scene of new industrial achievement on Anglesey is the nuclear power station at Wylfa, on the north coast, started at the beginning of 1964 and due to supply electricity into the national grid by the end of 1968. It is the world's most powerful nuclear power station, its reactor buildings will rise 150 feet above ground level and the station will have an electrical power output of 1,180,000 kilowatts. Like two of its predecessors in the Magnox or Calder Hall family of nuclear stations, Wylfa is being built for the Central Electricity Generating Board by the English Electric, Babcock & Wilcox, Taylor Woodrow Atomic Power Group. One of the most interesting constructional features is the use of pre-stressed spherical concrete pressure vessels. These are the largest yet built, with an internal diameter of ninety six feet, and round each steel liner there is an eleven foot thick concrete shell threaded through with 3,000 miles of wire cable, which is tensioned to give a vessel of immense strength. During construction work at Wylfa the scene has been one of a 'forest' of tower and gantry cranes—including the 400-ton crane Goliath—and Scotch derricks.

To build Wylfa, some 3,500 feet of tunnelling have been driven through the rock at a depth ranging from 100 feet at the pumphouse to fifty feet below sea level at the intake. When complete 53,000,000 gallons of water an hour will flow through the system.

At times during its construction, Wylfa has provided work for 2,000 men, many locally recruited. Five hundred of them at present live in a hutted camp built on site and provided with accommodation so that two men share twin-bedded rooms, and hot and cold running water. They have a canteen offering a full service, including breakfasts, lunches, suppers, as well as snack meals for men working irregular duties; a bar and cinema; skittle alley and soccer pitch; and two churches, each with its own resident chaplain.

When it became certain that a station was to be built at Wylfa, the churches in the area discussed how best to serve a new situation. It was decided that a full-time Chaplain should be appointed, and it was seen that this should and could only be done ecumenically. A committee representing the Anglican (Church in Wales), Baptist, Congregational, Methodist and Presbyterian Churches was formed and financial support secured from the various church courts.

The Rev. A. M. Roberts—a man who had been an engineer in Manchester and the Midlands before he became a minister—was appointed Chaplain and early in 1964 moved with his family into a house on the Council estate built for Wylfa workers. The work done by this Chaplain, and by his Roman Catholic colleague Father J. A. Taaffe, has attracted wide attention—including an excellent on-site television broadcast. This is how Mr. Roberts tells the story himself :

It was very clear that my first task was to listen and to learn something of the special world of civil engineering and construction camps. A great help in this has been the freedom granted me to visit all parts of the work site to meet men under working conditions. This I regard as the basis of all my work. Men cannot be served in a vacuum, and a Chaplain needs to be, as far as possible, a part of the society he tries to serve. I have tried to meet men at all levels in main and sub-contractors, management and unions although, on such a large and constantly changing site, this can be difficult.

The labour camp is the home of 600 of the key 'travelling men' characteristic of the construction industry. These are the men who bring their experience and skill to new projects and then move on to the next. In the camp I pay a personal visit to all non-Roman Catholic men as they move in; this usually entails meeting thirty or more new men per week. . . . I try (adds

Chaplain Roberts) to make it clear that I am not interested only in Church people—or indeed in Church attendance—but that my wish is to be of service in any way I can.

Our small Church in the camp—beautifully constructed by the site craftsmen—is not well attended . . . the congregation, constantly changing, as men come and go, is usually between fifteen and twenty, with an occasional stronger gathering for Sacrament or Thanksgiving service. Serving various nationalities and Churches as we do, the form of service is a compromise which is far from ideal. Yet men of many races have worshipped and found real fellowship together. Those who do come are extremely faithful.

The Rev. Roberts concludes his story by mentioning a small study group which meets at his home 'to study something of the particular characteristics of the construction industry and the social consequences of industrialisation . . . perhaps we are being too ambitious, but the members are keen and I take it to be part of the responsibility of a Chaplain to attempt to help industry as a social structure to an understanding of itself, its values, dimensions and obligations'.

Apart from the hundreds of men living on site, workers at present travel by special buses to Wylfa from all over the island. When construction has finished, there will still be jobs for several hundred men—and not all merely as what Captain Alex Robertson, a former chairman of Anglesey County Council, has called 'hewers of wood and drawers of water'. Anglesey wants (says Capt. Robertson), and is getting at places like Wylfa, the type of industry giving local people opportunities for promotion and using their traditional skill and intelligence in positions of responsibility.

The County Council has maintained close contact with the electricity authorities to ensure that adequate facilities were available to train young people through joint ventures between the Central Electricity Generating Board and Anglesey's Education Committee. During the construction of Wylfa the Electricity Board has, in fact, run a Training Centre where apprentice technicians are being taught for eventual appointment as station operational staff.

Anglesey needs new industry of many kinds, quite apart from a national project on the Wylfa scale, but not 'at any price'. This the County Council recognises and it deserves high praise for its sense of balance in the difficult decisions which have to be made in giving or denying industrial planning permission. In recognising the fact that Anglesey is not traditionally an industrialised county and that possible new industries must be looked at in the light of the effect they might have on the island's cultural life, its farming and its profitable tourist trade, the authority's decisions are not popular with everyone.

There was, for instance, the decision in December, 1964 when Anglesey County Council agreed with its Planning Committee that an oil refinery suggested for Holyhead should not be allowed. The outcry was immediate, mainly from trade union leaders and people outside the island saying that far from helping to better themselves the people of Anglesey were stifling development and keeping work away.

The County's decision had to be made in the light of approval for the idea of giving up 1,000 acres of good farm land for an oil refinery, approval which came from the county town itself—Beaumaris (at the other end of the island from the proposed refinery site), from Holyhead (provided, they said the refinery's tall buildings did not in any way prejudice the R.A.F. Station at Valley), and—naturally enough—from British Railways (who have a vested interest in Holyhead as a port).

The industries Anglesey has attracted do not, as might an oil refinery, constitute any threat to air purity. Anglesey-made goods include vehicle bodies, light naval craft, clothing, toys, clocks, food products and boats. Incidentally, when a new factory moved into Llangefni from Staffordshire it was announced by the Liverpool *Daily Post* that 'it will initially employ seventy people, most of them in the manufacture of pneumatic *calves* of high quality and precision'. (For calves, please read valves!)

At Beaumaris the Saro Company, who provide work for nearly 1000 people, make a wide range of products from radio telescope reflectors to floating pontoon bridges, and the firm has had a century's experience in building marine craft—particularly small high-speed Naval vessels. This Anglesey factory, part of the Hawker Siddeley Group, was built on the site of a Fransiscan priory founded in 1237, and during the war was busy on conversion and maintenance of flying boats. After the war, and until 1953, the company—renamed Saunders Engineering & Shipyard Limited—turned to making motor bus bodies, over

Wooden spoons carved in the 17th century by young Welshmen as love tokens, romantic bygones now eagerly sought by collectors.

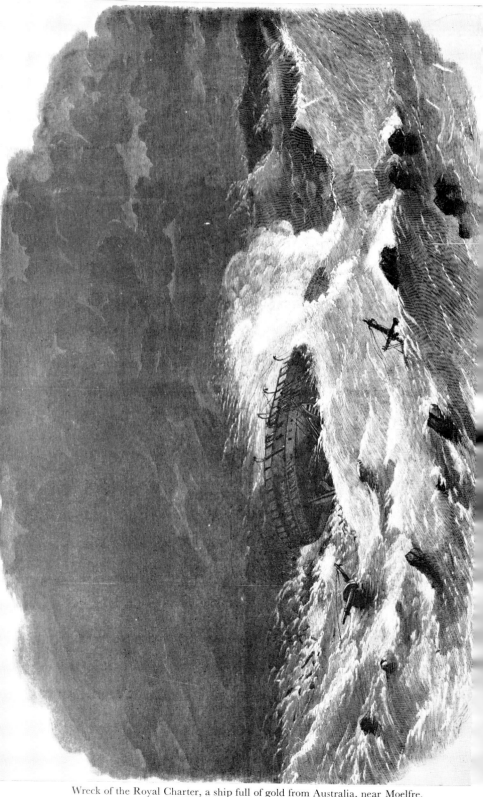

Wreck of the Royal Charter, a ship full of gold from Australia, near Moelfre,
on the 26th of October, 1859.

1,300 of which were built in the best traditional way of local craftsmen and are now worked in far-off places like Cuba, the Gold Coast and New Zealand. Three hundred double-deckers were also built for London Transport.

In 1948, the marine side of the company, whose boat-building history dates from 1830, produced the world's first aluminium fast patrol boat for the Royal Navy, and patrol boats from Beaumaris are working in the navies of Japan, Burma and Finland. Other shipping built here includes inshore minesweepers and landing craft, as well as pleasure boats—and the famous Bluebird and Miss England II record-breaking speedboats.

As a company within the Hawker Siddeley Group, Saro (Anglesey) Limited was later merged with Gloster Equipment Limited of Gloucester, under the name of Gloster Saro Limited, and last year this firm was itself merged with the Birkenhead shipping firm of Cammell Lairds.

Another, but very different, industrial story of successful peacetime devlopment after the war happened at Holyhead. In 1943, at Beach Yard Works, a London company known as A. Wells & Company Limited, began making scientific instruments for the forces, and when the war ended turned to making alarm clocks. The company became known as the Anglesey Instrument and Clock Company; its product, alarm clocks.

The change-over was a huge project carried out under the direction of the late Mr. A. W. J. Wells—a man who started business after the first world war, making toys in North London. The Beach Yard Works were soon found too small and in 1946 Lady Megan Lloyd George officially opened a new 60,000 square feet factory at Kingsland, Holyhead. The tools, jigs and scientific parts used for clock making—all these had to be specially made. The job was done in nine months, after which begun the training of unskilled labour drawn from the villages of Anglesey.

For some years alarm clocks poured from the Holyhead factory, but competition was growing from increased imports of foreign clocks. Mr. Wells, again took up his first trade— making toys, this time in plastics. And again Anglesey craftsmanship paid off; by 1961—with hardware and fancy goods added to the output of toys and clocks—another factory extension was opened. The Wells firm likes to stress that all this has been achieved by private enterprise and Anglesey workmanship—'not one penny of Government money in the factory'.

Small, local industries in Anglesey are flourishing, with their products and services in much demand, and they appear to be sharing in the county's new prosperity. In one year recently the Anglesey Rural Community Council helped a number of concerns to find new premises and the necessary technical advice, including a light textile company, fabricating and welding industry, a cabinet maker, two boatyards and a potter.

The Anglesey Rural Community Council is enterprising enough to see that a frequently neglected aspect of small industries is business administration. Office work can mean much waste of time and money unless efficient methods are employed, and to help raise standards the Council started a Business Management Course.

New industries have come, some old ones have gone. One that closed when the war began in 1939 had flourished around Newborough Warren for nearly 400 years. It was the making of mats, ropes, baskets, and various fancy goods from the local marram grass and was mainly carried on by women.

Vast quantities of sand were first blown over the area in the year 1331, at the Feast of St. Nicholas, and in a storm which lasted for a fortnight farms and buildings were buried beneath vast quantities of sand. During the reign of Elizabeth I, marram grass was planted to prevent further movement of the coastal sands and it was then that the local industry started. The custom was for the workers to rent plots on the warren from the owners at anything between ten shillings to two pounds a year, and grass was cut from August to November with a specially shaped sickle. Even the children were able to earn some money out of the marram grass industry by collecting stones (the best of which came from Malldraeth Cob) for sharpening the sickles. After cutting, the grass was tied up in a pyramid-shaped bundle and left to ripen for two or three weeks until it was almost white in colour. Later, large numbers of sheaves were stacked together and thatched. When it came to plaiting, eight Welsh yards (of 40 inches each) made a thong or lace (carrai) and eight thongs were needed to make one mat—but the women were fast and one of the best operators was reported as normally doing 64 Welsh yards in a day.

There were many uses for the mats. One was for floor covering, sometimes for churches as at Newborough, Beaumaris and Llandisilio. Other church uses for the manufactured products of marram grass were buffets and hassocks. On the farm there were many uses—covering seed frames, strawberry matting and ropes for thatching. For the sportsman, nets and cordage. Even in the copper mines of Parys Mountain a use was found for the grass—as a filter during the processes of washing copper ore. The suppliers were usually paid with token coins and some of these were found only twenty or so years ago among some ruins in Newborough Warren.

Since Newborough was common land all went well for the peasants until its enclosure in 1815. One hundred acres were then allotted to the poor but since they were unable to afford to pay certain assessments, the land was sold. It was through the Enclosures Act, and competition from other products used for mat and rop making, that the industry suffered badly in the 19th century. However, it managed to survive in a small way, and by 1913 something of a revival was brought about by forming a matmakers' association on a co-operative basis. Its founder, Colonel Cotton, of Plas Gwyn, Llanfair P.G., secured business with big seed growing firms, as well as with various agricultural suppliers. As a business, this ancient craft was, however, finally finished in 1939.

The windmill—and in certain places the watermill—have been important Anglesey workshops. The earliest (there is a reference to one in Newborough in 1303) were made of wood and were called postmills or pegmills, because the whole structure turned on a vertical post so that the mill faced the wind from whichever direction it came. Later, the roof alone revolved and other mechanical improvements followed.

The mills came into prominence because, on a flat island like Anglesey, there was not much force in the running water and in a dry summer, water was scarce. In the summer of 1741, for instance, it was recorded that 'all the watermills have dried up'. Again, in 1868, there are records of cattle dying of thirst on the island and sixpence a quart being paid in Holyhead for water. The mills declined rapidly in the latter years of the 19th century, unable to compete with modern steam mills in the towns on the mainland, despite the fact that it was an offence for a baker to purchase flour 'from such towns as Liverpool to the trading detriment of the mills of Anglesey'.

Another island industry, but never of major importance, is fishing. In 1775 reference was made to the big contribution played by herrings in the diet of the poor, but after the failure of this source of food 'the potato has been much planted and has become a principal food of the inhabitants'. From living 'chiefly on this esculent and not salted herrings' was considered by another chronicler to have been the reason for a 'great increase of people on this isle'.

However moribund the fishing industry eventually became round the coasts of Anglesey the fact remains that in the middle of the 18th century fish were regarded as being among the most profitable and abundant natural products of the area, and were listed at the time as including 'Cod, salmon, herring, ling, ray, haddock, plaice, whiting, sea-tench, turbot, soles, and flounders. Likewise oysters, crabs, lobsters, shrimps, prawns, with muscles and cockles in abundance'.

Oyster beds around the coasts of Anglesey are believed to have been an attraction to the Roman invaders, and earlier writers frequently referred to the size and excellence of Anglesey oysters. For instance, at Penmon in the 18th century the harbour was reported as having 'plenty of oysters, remarkably large. The poor find constant employment in the dredge and in pickling the fish for foreign consumption'.

Large quantities of oysters were pickled each year, packed in small casks and sent to different parts of the United Kingdom, but the industry, centred on Rhoscolyn, finally died out with the exhaustion of the oyster beds.

IX

COPPER RUSH

Of the basic industries, apart from agriculture, two others—mining and quarrying—were at one time of considerable size and interest, particularly mining for copper at Parys Mountain, in the north-east corner of the island. This is a desolate, eerie hill 480 feet high, from where—150 years ago—the output of copper was so great that it controlled the world price.

The hill itself is composed of striking formations of shale and quartz, and originally—as early as Roman times—the copper ore was obtained partly by picking, partly by blasting. It was impure ore and to clear it from sulphur the ore was burnt between two long parallel walls forming beds of copper—as much as 2,000 tons of ore at a time which would take up to ten months to burn. A richer produce of copper was, however, obtained from the water lodged in the bottom of the bed or from ore which was drawn up, either by winches or by windmills, to the surface and then distributed into rectangular pits containing iron refuse. The particles of copper were precipitated by the iron which then gradually dissolved into a yellow ochre. Although the mines are not now worked, yellow ochre is still obtained from the copper deposits.

Not only was copper obtained from Parys Mountain, but also some lead and silver. Today, the scene is a sombre one, a relic of past industrial activity which, two years ago, was given a book to itself—'The Copper Mountain' by John Rowlands and published by the Anglesey Antiquarian Society.

To the summit, Parys Mountain is covered with huge piles of debris. Ugly, perhaps; but strangely attractive in its silence, its 'atmosphere' of human toil and hope, its magnificent colours from greens and browns to blues and purples (so lovely that I had the scene painted in oils for me by Elwyn Roberts, a local artist).

In recent years the Atomic Energy Division of the Government's Geological Survey and Museum carried out some prospecting at Parys Mountain for uranium, but found none.

Still more recently other forms of prospecting have been carried out which may or may not prove that copper mining could again be a business proposition and with it the production of copper goods in the Amlwch area. In this hope, a new factor of considerable help could be the abundant and possibly cheap electric power from the nearby Wylfa nuclear power station.

No copper mining appears to have been carried on at Parys Mountain between the Roman period and the 18th century, but local inhabitants continued to talk about a 'pool of copper-water' and eventually, in 1757, an Anglesey landowner, Sir Nicholas Bayley (an ancestor of the Marquess of Anglesey) started explorations. He found no copper. Five years later a Scot landed in Anglesey in curious circumstances. His name was Alexander Frazier, reported to have fled Scotland on account of a criminal charge. It appears he was trying to make his way across the Irish Sea when he was shipwrecked and found refuge on Anglesey. How, it does not seem to be known, but he met and made friends with Sir Nicholas Bayley. The forceful Scot had before long persuaded his new friend to a renewed effort to find copper ore. They did—although, soon after the start, there was a break in profitable operations on account of flooding.

If Alexander Frazier can be called the discoverer of what were to become great riches, he does not seem to have gained much himself—in its way, what might be called 'big business' moved in and by 1764 there are records of 'a company of smelters', Roe & Co., of Cheshire, getting a twenty-one year lease from Sir Nicholas Bayley. The great day in the subsequent history of Parys Mountain came on March 2nd, 1768. It was on this day, after previous abortive shafts had been sunk, that the adventurers struck lucky. They decided to take three points along a north and south line across the middle of the hill. No sooner had a mere seven feet been excavated than ore was struck in tremendous quantities. The Copper Rush had begun.

What had been a hamlet of six houses in 1766 became, by the turn of the century, a thriving town of 6,000 people, a source of wealth and of economic importance to the United Kingdom export trade and last, but not least, the scene of much human drama. On this score T. Rowland Hughes (1903-49) wrote a piece about Parys Mountain called 'Grinding Poverty' from which I quote this description of conditions:

'After my grandfather married, he brought his wife, a girl from Pensarn, home to live in the little cottage, and there his two children, my father and Uncle Huw, were born, to be brought up in great poverty, despite my grandparents' ceaseless toil. To my grandmother fell the task of tending the two cows, two pigs and three dozen chickens on the homestead, while her husband was employed in the Parys Mountain Copper Mines, where he had started work at the age of eight for a wage of fourpence for a twelve-hour day. He was only twelve when he went down below to mine copper, and there he toiled like a galley-slave for the rest of his life. On many a settling-up Saturday he used to return home without a halfpenny to bless himself with, after a whole month of accursedly hard toil; for the owners followed a system of "stoppages" against the cost of candles, powder, sharpening augers and hoisting the ore from the mine. There were times, indeed, when my grandfather returned home, at the month's end, actually in debt to his owners, since this shameful levy totalled more than the wage he had earned in a month of sweated, sweltering labour underground. My grandmother tried to induce him to give up the work, but they could not make a living out of the homestead with its three small, mean fields, and food had to be provided for themselves and their two children.

'So, day by day, and week by week, my unfortunate grandfather had to go down the Coronation shaft, to kill himself in the effort to provide for his little family. And every morning at six, in the Prayer Meeting that was held in the smithy on the surface, he gave thanks to God that he was able to keep his children from starvation.'

The Parys Mountain mines became the most productive in Europe. They employed 1,500 men and women (the latter known as Copper Ladies) and turned out something like 3,000 tons of metallic copper every year. Amlwch, now once again only a fishing village, became a prosperous port. Its harbour facilities were enlarged to cope with the profitable export of ore, but even then ships had to queue up at Holyhead before they could get into Amlwch. In this Copper Age, hard lead ores from the mine were not thought worth smelting—they went to make a road, an expensive one at that, from the Mountain to Amlwch port.

Besides copper, this is the rich list of minerals which scientists identified from Parys Mountain :

Alum	Chalcopyrite	Minimom
Anglesite	Chlorite	Pyrite
(see reference	Coppers	Quartz
below)	Calena	Selenite
Asbestos	Haematite	Serpentine
Barytos	Hydro-glockerite	Silver
Blende	Malachite	Sulphur
Chalcanthite	Melaconite	Tetrahedrite
Chalcocite	Melanterite	White Mica

There were, in all, twelve separate lodes charted at Parys Mountain. Of these, what is known as the Great Lode turned out also to be the most productive in terms of copper. Not only that, but one 19th century writer recorded that above the copper ore, less than a yard below the soil, was a bed of yellowish clay containing lead ore then worth over £600 a ton. It was, however, found difficult to smelt and something like 8,000 tons was thrown out on to the banks. On these same banks a rare mineral has been found, or at least small white crystals of it. This is Anglesite, a beautiful crystaline mineral so named because it was first found on Parys Mountain.

Apart from that enterprising Scotsman Mr. Alexander Frazier, and the company of smelters from Cheshire, Cornishmen played a leading part in the development of the copper mines. According to Mr. John Rowlands, an assistant director of education for Anglesey and to whose book I referred earlier in the chapter, the Mona Mine or Parys Mountain was administratively a Cornish colony, and in particular, the concern of the Treweek family.

A Cornish copper miner's son James Henry Treweek, and his family, arrived at Amlwch during October, 1811, the year in which the Vivian Company of Swansea, took a lease of Mona Mine, owned by Lord Anglesey, of Plas Newydd. James Treweek came to Anglesey as the Vivian Company mine agent, and in due course, aroused considerable local criticism and antagonism. He brought other Cornishmen to the county to assist with the mine administration, and was immediately accused of nepotism.

Treweek learned Welsh and became a Wesleyan lay-preacher, although most of his sermons were in English. He served on public bodies and concerned himself in the welfare of the district, but although he was well regarded at Plas Newydd his enemies never relented.

In time, of course, even the rich lodes of Parys became exhausted. Solid mining came to an end just before the turn of this century. For a time it was considered worthwhile to pick over the old spoil-banks; even the peat of nearby bogs has been burned and copper taken from the ashes.

Today, the visitor is adequately warned by notice boards of one kind or another of the dangers of walking or driving up the winding rock-strewn tracks of the abandoned mountain. In many places the tracks themselves run at a torturous angle, overhanging vast pits below; and even more dangerous, fallen debris hides hidden shafts. But to go there is immensely rewarding. At one time, vast underground caverns could be entered and 'with a candle (as the geologist Greenly wrote) display a scene of intense brilliancy—some of it no doubt due to the quartz in the rock face. Near the summit of the hill itself, is in fact a great boss of quartz rock known as "Careg-y-doll"—the crag of the toll-taking.

There are other small-scale quarrying and mining activities on Anglesey. One of these is the supply of pure quartz for the potteries of Staffordshire. Quartzites in the Gwna series of rocks are quarried at various places—including Pen-y-Parc, Beaumaris.

In building operations, native rock has been used to quite a large extent, and big pieces of the evenly-splitting rocks of the Mona complex were used in making the great breakwater at Holyhead, more than a mile and a half long, sixty feet wide and forty feet high. There are on the island a number of old lime kilns, and here and there even a few signs of old brick works—although bricks as a building material had been very little used in Anglesey.

Coal measures in Anglesey have been known for hundreds of years. A licence to mine coal was granted by the Crown to Llewelyn ap Rhys ap Tudor as early as 1450. There are certain references to coal mining in Anglesey in the first half of the 17th century, and in the year 1810 some local farmers sank a pit near Glantreath. It was not good quality coal, but it was mined for many years. Between about 1850 and 1875 coal pits were worked at Morfa-mawr, but since then—despite many other test borings—no appreciable quantity of coal seems to have been obtained.

X

FOLKLORE

MAGIC—IN LEGEND

To the Cymry and the pure Kelt the past
is at their elbows continually . . . other races
forfeit infancy, forfeit youth and manhood
with their progression to the wisdom age
may bestow. These have each stage always
alive . . . they have poetry in them; they are
valiant; they are hospitable to teach the
Arab a lesson.

—George Meredith (1828-1909)

A ll Wales, Anglesey very much included, is rich in story and
legend, in its own poetry and romantic prose. Much of it is
written for, or heard at, the annual assembly of musical
and literary talent known as the eisteddfod; again, some of the
tales have simply been recounted in the homes of the people
from one generation to another.

Anglesey's historical reputation as a land of poets is still
being maintained. Three years ago, at the National eisteddfod
held at Newtown, it was an island farmer—Mr. Tom Parri-Jones
—who won the National Eisteddfod Crown for a play called
'The Flies', written under the pen-name of Aristoffanes
and which emulated the Greek poet to show the dilemma of
mankind in the nuclear age. This farmer writer also won the
Crown five years ago, at Llandudno, and has won the Chair
and the Prose Medal. Mr. Parri-Jones is, like so many before
him, an intelligent, sensitive and independent poet, with a
ready feeling for what is noble and distinguished.

A Welsh 'sitting' session of bards is how the dictionary
prosaically describes the eisteddfod. The real spirit of these
colourful gatherings of the nations of the world met, not to argue
around conference tables as statesmen and politicians, but as

writers and musicians to share their arts, is captured in poetry
by Sir Lewis Morris (1833-1907):

'AT THE EISTEDDFOD'

The close-ranked faces rise,
With their watching, eager eyes,
And the banners and the mottoes blaze above :
And without, on either hand,
The eternal mountains stand,
And the salt sea river ebbs and flows again,
And through the thin-drawn bridge the wandering winds
    complain.
Here is the Congress met,
The bardic senate set,
And young hearts flutter at the voice of fate;
All the fair August day
Song echoes, harpers play,
And on the unaccustomed ear the strange
Penillion rise and fall through change and counter-change.
Oh Mona, land of song!
Oh mother of Wales! how long
From thy dear shores an exile have I been!
Still from thy lonely plains,
Ascend the old sweet strains,
And at the mine, or plough, or humble home,
The dreaming peasant hears diviner music come
This innocent, Peaceful strife,
This struggle to fuller life,
Is still the one delight of Cymric souls—
Swell, blended rhythm! still
The gay pavilions fill.
Soar, of young voices, resonant and fair;
Still let the sheathed sword gleam above the bardic chair.

*

The Menai ebbs and flows,
And the song-tide wanes and goes,
And the singers and the harp-players are dumb;
The eternal mountains rise
Like the cloud upon the skies,
And my heart is full of joy for the songs that are still,

The deep sea and the soaring hills, and the steadfast Omnipotent Will.

* * *

Delicate, imaginative tales including much romance of Nature are typical of the literature of Wales . . . 'magic is just the word for it' (says Matthew Arnold in his 'Celtic Magic')— 'the magic of nature; not merely an honest smack of the soil, a faithful realism—that the Germans had; but the intimate life of Nature, her weird power and her fairy charm. . . .'

Arnold gives several examples of this Celtic emotional writing to illustrate its beauty. For instance, a description of Olwen —'more yellow was her hair than the flower of the broom, and her skin was whiter than the foam of the wave, and fairer were her hands and her fingers than the blossoms of the wood anemone amidst the spray of the meadow fountains'.

It is not, however, only in Celtic literature that 'magic' is an ingredient. It is also in the country's folklore; in its gipsy stories told to generations of nomadic children in waggons pitched from the heaths of Anglesey to the shores of Pembroke; and it is built into the superstitions of the island fishermen, sailors and men of the land. Little of these tales has been published, and such rare books as there are in existence have become collectors' pieces. In 1913, for instance, the Gregynog Press—sponsored by the philanthropists Gwendoline and Margaret Davies, sisters of Lord Davies of Llandinam—produced a volume entitled *XXI Welsh Gipsy Folk Tales,* collected by John Sampson (himself a gipsy) with engravings on wood by Agnes Miller Parker.

This fascinating book was a limited edition of 250 copies only. Copies numbered 1–15 in mustard-yellow levant morocco were eight guineas, the other 235 were in mustard-yellow Welsh sheepskin, at three guineas. One was sold by Francis Edwards of Marylebone High Street, London, for £22 in July 1961. The Gregynog Press closed down in 1940 and binding of the last unfinished volumes were done in the National Library of Wales in 1952.

Fairies figure often in Anglesey tales and, according to one authority — Edmund Jones (1702–93) of Aberystwyth — an 'abundance of people saw them (the fairies) and heard their musick, which everyone said was low and pleasant, but none could ever learn the tune. Heard their talking like that of many talking together, but the words seldom heard. But to those who did hear, they seemed to dispute much about future events, and about what they were to do; whence it came to a proverb in the parish concerning disagreeing persons. *Ni chytunant hwy mwy na bendith y mamau,* i.e., they will not more agree than the fairies.

'They appeared diverse ways, but their most frequent way of appearing was like dancing companies with musick, and in the form of funerals. When they appeared like dancing companies, they were desirous to entice persons into their company, and some were drawn among them and remained among them some time; usually a whole year, as did Edmund William Rees, a man whom I well knew, and was a neighbour, who came back at the year's end, and looked very bad. But either they were not able to give much account of themselves or they durst not give it, only said they had been dancing, and that the time was short. . . . It was the general opinion in times past, when these things were more frequent, that the fairies knew whatever was spoken in the air without the houses, not so much what was spoken in the houses. I suppose they chiefly knew what was spoken in the air at night. It was also said that they rather appeared to an uneven number of persons—to one, three, five, etc., and oftener to men than to women.'

Another author, P. H. Emerson, an Englishman, set up home in Anglesey in the 1890's for the sole purpose of writing down traditional stories just as they were told. The former London evening paper, the *Pall Mall Gazette,* was highly enthusiastic over these tales which are mainly domestic, many dealing with making and losing money and the various trials of running a household; others have some mention of fairies 'wearing short dresses, with hair in a plaited pigtail down the back'.

Emerson describes how the fairy stories were passed around the island 'before the Reformation, when the Christian world was enveloped in Popish darkness and superstition . . . and such a swarm of idle people, under the name of minstrels, poets, begging friars, etc., were permitted to ramble about . . . such people might, at appointed times on fine moonlight nights, assemble in some sequestered spot, to regulate their dark affairs and divide the spoil; and then perform their nightly orgies, so as to terrify people from coming near them, lest their tricks and cheats should be discovered. It is possible the men of Ystrad might have less superstition, and somewhat more courage, than their neighbours, and supposing such a one to come suddenly on these nightly revellers, he would of course cause great consternation amongst them; and, on finding a comely female in the group, it is not unnatural to imagine that he might, as the heroes of old have done before him, seize on a beauteous Helen, carry her home, and in process of time marry her—for many valorous knights have done the latter; but she, on account of some domestic jars, might afterwards have eloped from him, and returned to her former companions and occupation.'

Emerson's book of 1894, perhaps the only one of its kind, is long since out of print, but the stories that follow are among the most typical.

*　　*　　*　　*

THE FAIRIES' MINT

Once upon a time there was a miller, who lived in Anglesey. One day he noticed that some of his sacks had been moved during the night. The following day he felt sure that some of his grain had been disturbed, and, lastly, he was sure someone had been working his mill in the night during his absence. He confided his suspicions to a friend, and they determined to go the next night and watch the mill. The following night, at about midnight, as they approached the mill that stood on a bare stony hill, they were surprised to find the mill all lit up and at work, the great sails turning in the black night. Creeping up softly to a small window, the miller looked in, and saw a crowd of little men carrying small bags, and emptying them into the millstones. He could not see, however, what was in the bags, so he crept to another window, when he saw golden coins coming from the mill, from the place where the flour usually ran out.

Immediately the miller went to the mill door, and, putting his key in the lock, he unlocked the door; and as he did so the lights went out suddenly, and the mill stopped working. As he and his friend went into the dark mill they could hear sounds of people running about, but by the time they lit up the mill again there was nobody to be seen, but scattered all about the millstones and on the floor were cockle-shells.

After that, many persons who passed the mill at midnight

94

said they saw the mill lit up and working, but the old miller left the fairies alone to coin their money.

*   *   *   *

MOTHER KADDY

Mother Kaddy sat in her cottage in Love Lane, cutting the cards, for she was a witch they said; certainly she had a black cat and a jackdaw who could talk better than a parrot, but the jackdaw spoke only in Welsh. Kaddy was a tall, thin, black-eyed, yellow-skinned woman, with the curious furtive and cunning eyes of all the old beldames who affect magic.

It was September and Kaddy knew her practice would be good during that month, for in April and September the Welsh maidens are particularly sensitive to the influence of magic. Indeed, you may see them upon the full moon night of these months going up to the old sexton in a body at midnight, each giving him a sixpence to allow them to have the key to the church door. He hands the key to one and she unlocks the door at the stroke of twelve, and placing the key on her right finger she walks inside, followed by her friends, who produce wedding rings, borrowed from their married friends, and place them on their middle fingers, when they form in line and proceed round the church, turning the ring at the finish of every round and wishing. After having marched thrice round the church, they come forth, having spoken never a word, lock the door and go home, the leader of the girls taking the key with her and sleeping with it under her pillow, when she dreams of her future love. The next morning she returns the key to the sexton.

That season the full moon was drawing nearer, and Kaddy sat in her cottage reading an old Welsh book, when a dark-eyed, slim girl, Isabella, knocked at the door.

'Come in, dear,' said Kaddy, without moving. 'Well, dear, what can I do for you?'

'Well, indeed, mother, please to tell me how I'm to know if the young man I'm courting close with loves me.'

'What, young Robert Roberts, dear?'

'Yes to be sure, Kaddy, but who will have told you?'

'I know, dear, I know; the cards tell me and so does the bird; he goes everywhere and is sure to see everything. Well, dear, I'll tell you, but you must pay half-a-crown first.'

95

Isabella placed the money on the table.

'Well, dear, do you on Michaelmas night, when you go to bed, get a threepenny ball of yarn, and after you have opened your bedroom window throw the ball as far as you can, but keep hold of one end of the yarn. Then you must say out loud, "Whoever comes to catch this ball and tugs at it, let him be my sweetheart." Then you must begin to reel it up, dear, and if young Robert Roberts loves you he'll come and tug at it, or if anybody else comes, they'll tug at it.'

'Oh, thank you, Kaddy.'

'Well, now child, go, for I've some friends coming.'

Isabella had scarce got down the street before four laughing, black-eyed girls burst in and began chattering in Welsh, the jackdaw joining in the babel.

'See, Kaddy, there's two shillings—sixpence from each of us,' said one.

'And, Kaddy, here's a paper of buns.'

'And here's a quarter of a pound of fine tea.'

'And see, Kaddy, here will be the sugar,' said the fourth. 'We want the tea fortune.'

'Well, well, girls, I suppose I shall have to please you. Sit down and make yourselves comfortable whilst I brew the tea.'

Old Kaddy raised her long lank body and busied herself making the tea and setting the table. When everything was ready they drank their tea with much fun and chaff and after the meal was finished at a signal from Kaddy each girl turned her cup upside down upon her saucer. Kaddy then drew the nearest cup towards her, and raising it she looked at the careless arrangement of tea leaves to try and see what figure they suggested, for this is the practice of the tea fortune.

'There's a letter coming for you, Eva; I see a postman,' said Kaddy.

Then she took the second cup.

'You will have money, Nellie; I see gold.'

And to the third, 'I see a black man with a beard; you'll go foreign, Jennie.'

And to the fourth, 'You'll marry a light-haired man and he will treat you well.'

Then the girls babbled and old Kaddy silently rocked herself to and fro until they left, chattering like starlings, when Kaddy put the shillings in a box.

...or whom the bell tolls . . . buried here at Llanallgo Church are 140 bodies from the wreck of the Royal Charter, men weighed down in the sea by the gold they were carrying home from Australia.

To build Wylfa, the world's most powerful nuclear power station, over three thousand feet
tunnelling have been driven one hundred feet deep through the rock.

The evening was cool and she had piled on more coals, for Kaddy lived well: her practice was lucrative.

'Ay, ay, there is a stranger coming,' said Kaddy, for a thin bit of burnt coal sticking to the bars was waving towards her— a bit of cinder resembling a slip of silk.

It was now dusk, and Kaddy knew well that all the graver persons and more serious cases came to her at that hour, so she did not light her lamp.

Presently there was a knock at the door, and in response to Kaddy's invitation a fat woman, breathing hard, entered and sat herself down uninvited.

'Well, Mrs. Williams, what's the matter?'

'Oh, I'm bewitched, Kaddy.'

'Toots; how is that, Lizzie?'

'Yes, I'm bewitched, everything goes wrong with me, and I want you to take off the spell.'

'Well, Lizzie, to be sure I will, but you must pay five shillings first.'

"Well, Kaddy, I will,' and she threw the shillings on the table.

'Have you got any enemies?'

'I don't know of anybody, and yet I think I do.'

'Who is it?'

'Well, to be sure, it might be Nellie Brag, she's envious.'

'Now, Lizzie, do you look at her tomorrow. If it should be her I'll put a mark on her, and I'll find out tonight by the cards; but if it isn't her, and you'll know by her having no mark, it must be old Shan Jones with the evil eye. Now mind next time you pass old Shan, don't look her in the face, but look down at her feet till you are past. When you've seen her, go home and put seven pins in a cork, and get up and next morning early before the crows go over to Caernarvon, and stay till they have gone over, but don't look at them as they go over; and when you think they have all gone, go home, and do the same thing in the evening and do it for three days; and on the third day at dusk go round to Shan's house and hide close by and watch till you see somebody go in or come out, and directly you see the door open throw the cork with the pins into the passage, and then you'll be cured and you won't feel any more of the evil eye.'

'God is good, Kaddy; I hope it will be sure to come true.'

97

'Do as I tell you, Lizzie, do as I tell you. Good-night.'

When Lizzie had gone, old Kaddy's lean, yellow features lighted up, and smiling to herself she said, patting her cat—'Nine and six, nine and six. Whatever!'

*   *   *   *

AT THE SIGN OF THE RING AND THE RAVEN

Poor Hugh Owen lived in a small croft on the bare hills of Anglesey, facing the sea. He had a hard struggle to support his wife and six children upon the limestone-based, grass-covered hollow with his small flock of sheep; for in addition to poverty he suffered tortures from rheumatism . . . moreover he had a very hard and exacting landlord over him.

In the springtime, after the cuckoos awoke from their long sleep, and the rooks assembled in a field to pair, Hugh's face brightened a little, for he eked out a precarious existence by nesting on the stony ledges and moors as the eggs fell in season —first for lapwings' eggs and later for puffins' eggs, which are nearly as good to eat : the gulls' eggs he used for cooking.

Upon one of these expeditions he found a raven's nest with four hatchlings, which he took home and tried to rear; but all died save the cock bird, which was brought up as a great family pet. But the bird had to be watched, for whenever opportunity offered he stole off with all bright objects and hid them underneath the old dresser; but these petty larcenies were forgiven him, for he would follow old Hugh like a dog, from tree to tree.

One day, Hugh was down in Beaumaris, and he found a piece of coal on the pavement. Picking it up he put it carefully in his pocket and took it home, afterwards always carrying it with him; for no Anglesey man must ever pass a piece of coal, but must carry it secretly till luck comes.

When he got home his wife ran out joyfully and said—

'Hugh, we are sure to have good luck—I dropped a fork on the floor at noon today.'

'Ie,' said Hugh, 'so did I drop a knife on the floor down at the "White Lion" at Beaumaris; but we'll see, for if good luck doesn't come, I must sell up everything to pay the rent,' finished Hugh, sitting down.

'Well, indeed, what's the news, Hugh ?'

'Oh, bad, bad, Kaddy. A lot of them cocklers have been

over to the Wailing Sands yesterday gathering cockles; there were fifteen of them and old Owen Owens and his son were running them home. They'd filled the boat with cockles and shiels (sprats) and she was low in the water, and a bit of breeze came up, and old Owen Owens would have them throw the cockles out, but Isabella Roberts wouldn't—you know she's a devil of a woman—so the boat capsized and everyone was drowned except old Owen's son. . . .'

'Dear, dear! that's a bad job.'

As they were talking there was a tapping at the window, and the pet raven appeared.

The black bird flew in and alighting on the table dropped something glistening thereupon. The eldest boy snatched it up and shouted—

'Why, it's a ring!'

Old Hugh arose quickly and took it from him, and looking at it carefully he saw arms cut in a bloodstone set in a large signet ring, but he was ignorant of heraldry. Replacing the ring on the table he went to the fireplace and threw the piece of coal slyly into the fire—the luck had come.

After having done this he put the ring in a place of safety and went to bed perplexed; for he was battling with his conscience whether he should take it to Bangor to sell or try and find the owner.

But the morning brought counsel, and he arose early and took the ring to the parson and told him the circumstances. The parson examined it carefully and said—

'Oh, yes, the arms are those of Lord Moelfre; he's sure to value the ring. If you leave it with me, I will restore it to him, and no doubt he will reward you for your honesty.'

Owen blushed at his thoughts of the previous night and went home.

The parson that very afternoon had his strong little Welsh pony put into his trap and drove over to Lord Moelfre's house, where he was admitted into his presence.

'Have you lost a ring, sir?' asked the parson.

'Why, bless my soul, yes! Do you know anything about it?'

'Yes, I've got it.'

'Have you indeed? Well, you've saved my life. Do you know I have to wear that ring once a year, and if I lose it I am doomed to die within the twelvemonth, and to show you how anxious I have been to find the ring, I have offered one hundred pounds reward for it; and the whole country-side have been in my covers hunting high and low, and even draining the ditches dry, for I suspect I lost it in the Green Willows cover last week when I was shooting pheasants.'

'Well, indeed, I'm glad you've got it, but you owe Hugh Owen thanks, not me.'

Whereupon the parson told the story of the raven. Lord Moelfre was interested in the story of the raven, but he merely enquired Hugh Owen's address and circumstances, and, thanking the parson they parted.

Next morning, as Hugh's family were at breakfast, old Owen dropped his knife and Mrs. Owen let her fork slip from her hand to the floor.

'We are sure to have strangers before noon,' they both agreed.

In the morning, sure enough, a liveried servant called at the croft on horseback leading a second saddled horse by the bridle. When the door was opened to him he asked to see Hugh Owen and the raven.

Hugh was called from the back where he was sawing wood, and meanwhile the groom got off his horse and came indoors. After Hugh came the raven and alighted on the table. When the groom saw him he threw down a guinea piece, which the raven seized immediately, and began to turn over and dancing with it in his strong bill.

'By God, he's a queer bird; but that guinea is not for him, but for the children, whilst Hugh Owen comes with me, and he must bring the bird for my lord to see.'

So they rode off to Moelfre Place, the raven perched upon Owen's shoulder.

When they arrived at the house the groom led the way to the study where his master was sitting at a table writing. When Hugh Owen and his bird were ushered in, Lord Moelfre arose and thanked Hugh for his honesty and patted the bird.

The groom then told him of his behaviour with the guinea, so Lord Moelfre pulled out a guinea, and tossed it on to the writing-table. Immediately the raven dashed at it, and picking it up turned it over and over and began dancing with delight.

'Well now,' said Lord Moelfre, 'here's a purse with a hundred pounds I promised as a reward for the finder of the ring;

but on May 13th next I will have something more for you, so look out for my groom on that day.'

Old Hugh went home delighted, and on November 13th, three weeks afterwards, he drove off to pay his rent with a light heart.

In the olden days all rents were paid yearly on November 13th, and afterwards the farmers and crofters collected at one of the inns for a jollification. On that night all were chaffing a hanger-on at the inn, one John Jones, who had been detected that day stealing a long string of tobacco. He possessed a large metal tobacco box into which he had put the end of the string of tobacco shutting the lid down tightly upon it, forgetting to cut off the long tail; so that when he went out of the shop the tobacco tail draggled after him, and before he turned the corner the shopkeeper detected the theft and running after him caught the tobacco string and jerked the box from his pocket. Whereupon John Jones got wrath, and there was a fight, in which John Jones lost his red metal tobacco box and all. John Jones would do anything for tobacco. He used to go and dig up potatoes at night in his neighbours' gardens and sell them for tobacco to the sailors on the foreign ships. He would collect snails, limpets, sweet clams and Pary's clams and cockles for the foreign sailors in exchange for tobacco. The farmers made high game of him and kept asking him how he'd liked the English Chapel service; for John had turned religious; and though he had never a word of English, he attended the service regularly, saying they were 'very nice and mild'.

But John Jones was to have his revenge that night; for he had hung a straw man with a hollow turnip head in which burnt a candle, on the haunted crooked oak; leaning over the road above the China Rock. As the first trap with six farmers, all fresh, drove home, they lowered their voices as they approached the haunted tree—where a man is said to have hung himself—but the horse saw the ghost and shied and bolted, capsizing the trap and breaking the legs of one of the passengers. There was a great to-do that night and the straw man was cut down; but John Jones only grinned to himself.

When Hugh Owen got home from the feasting he found his boy had brought in a lot of dead robins.

'What are they for?' asked Hugh of his wife.

'Why, Hugh, Tommy says old Pat at Moelfre says they kill

all the robins ever year upon the day of the battle of the Boyne; because the Irish were creeping up to the Saxons, who were asleep, but a divil of a robin began pecking at the Saxon drummer's drum and awoke him, and he saw the enemy and gave the alarm, so the Irish were beaten.'

'Toot, toot; it's the young birds killing the old ones,' said Hugh.

The following spring Hugh was delighted when the cuckoos awoke, like all the seven sleepers.

'Ie, he's hoarse,' he said, as he heard the first cuckoo; 'but he'll soon get a lot of eggs and then his voice will be clear.'

All that spring Hugh was happy, for he knew something good was coming, and even if a knife had fallen from the table at night I do not believe he would have been uneasy and keep a sharp look-out for the deadly enemy the omen warned him against; but no such thing happened, and the morning of the 13th May broke brightly.

When Hugh got up he caught his cat and looked at her eyes to tell the size of the moon, but he waited till noon to verify his observations, when he found the irides were round, and the moon therefore full; for this lunar observance was believed in by the Welsh as well as the Chinese.

In the afternoon the groom appears, leading a saddled horse as before, and amid great excitement took Hugh to the new inn, the 'Ring and the Raven', that Hugh heard had been refitted and done up by Lord Moelfre. The 'Ring and the Raven' was a comfortable wayside inn, standing in thirty acres of ground, the property of Lord Moelfre. The inn was formerly called the 'Wayfarer', but since its restoration it had been renamed and a beautiful sign hung over the door, a raven with a ring in its bill.

Upon arriving at the inn Lord Moelfre came forth, and when Hugh had alighted and made his obeisance, Lord Moelfre said—

'Hugh Owen, for your honesty I give you this inn and the land belonging to it, as a freehold property, and here are your deeds.'

One of the old farmers, a crusty old bachelor, who wore spectacles, was reading one day in the bar, when the raven hopped on to his shoulder and stole his spectacles from his very nose. The old man swore horrible Welsh oaths, but the wily bird had flown. When old Hugh heard of the loss, he watched his pet and traced him to his cache in the hollow tree, where he found a lot of bright objects hidden in as purposeless a way as a miser hides his useless hoard. When the raven's store was rifled he died; of grief, Hugh said; of shame, said his wife.

*   *   *   *

'THE ORIGIN OF THE WELSH'

Many years ago there lived several wild tribes round the King of Persia's city, and the king's men were always annoying and harassing them, exacting yearly a heavy tribute. Now these tribes, though very brave in warfare, could not hold their own before the Persian army when sent out against them so that they paid their yearly tribute grudgingly, but took revenge, whenever they could, upon travellers, to or from the city, robbing and killing them.

At last one of the tribesmen, a clever old chieftain, thought of a cunning plan whereby to defeat the Persians, and free themselves from the yearly tribute. And this was his scheme:

The wild wastes where these tribes lived were infested with large birds called Rohs, which were very destructive to human beings—devouring men, women and children greedily whenever they could catch them. Such a terror were they that the tribes had to protect their village with high walls, and they slept securely, for the Roh hunted by night. This old chieftain determined to watch the birds, and find out their nesting-places; so he had a series of towers built, in which the watchmen could sleep securely by night. These towers were advanced in whatever direction the birds were seen to congregate by night. The observers reported that the Roh could not fly, but ran very swiftly, being fleeter than any horse.

At length, by watching, their nesting-places were found in a sand plain, and it was discovered that those monstrous birds stole sheep and cattle in great numbers.

The chieftain then gave orders for the watchmen to keep on guard until the young birds were hatched, when they were commanded to secure fifty, and bring them into the walled town. The order was carried out, and one night they secured fifty young birds just out of the egg, and brought them to the town.

The old chieftain then told off fifty skilful warriors, a man

103

to each bird, to his son being allotted the largest bird. These warriors were ordered to feed the birds on flesh, and to train them for battle. The birds grew up as tame as horses. Saddles and bridles were made for them, and they were trained and exercised just like chargers.

When the next tribute day came round, the King of Persia sent his emissaries to collect the tax, but the chieftains of the tribes insulted and defied them so that they returned to the king, who at once sent forward his army.

The chieftain then marshalled his men, and forty-six of the Rohs were drawn up in front of the army, the chief getting on the strongest bird. The remaining four were placed on the right flank, and ordered at a signal to advance and cut off the army, should they retreat.

The Rohs had small scales, like those of a fish, on their necks and bodies, the scales being hidden under a soft hair, except on the upper half of the neck. They had no feathers except on their wings. So they were invulnerable except as to the eyes—for in those days the Persians only had bows and arrows, and light javelins. When the Persian army advanced, the Rohs advanced at lightning speed, and made fearful havoc, the birds murdering and trampling the soldiers under foot, and beating them down with their powerful wings. In less than two hours half the Persian army was slain, and the rest had escaped. The tribes returned to their walled towns, delighted with their victory.

When the news of his defeat reached the King of Persia he was wroth beyond expression, and could not sleep for rage. So the next morning he called for his magician.

'What are you going to do with the birds?' asked the king.

'Well, I've been thinking the matter over,' replied the magician.

Cannot you destroy all of them?'

'No, your Majesty, I cannot destroy them, for I have not the power; but I can get rid of them in one way; for though I cannot put out life, I have the power of turning one life into some other living creature.'

'Well, what will you turn them into?' asked the king.

'I'll consider tonight, your Majesty.'

The next day, at ten, the magician appeared before the king, who asked:

'Have you considered well?'

'Yes, your Majesty.'

'Well, how are you going to act?'

'Your Majesty, I've thought and thought during the night, and the best thing we can do is to turn all the birds into fairies.'

'What are fairies?' asked the king.

'I've planned it all out, and I hope your Majesty will agree.'

'Oh! I'll agree, as long as they never molest us more.'

'Well, your Majesty, I'm going to turn them to fairies—small living creatures to live in caves in the bowels of the earth, and they shall only visit people living on earth once a year. They shall be harmless, and hurt nothing; they shall be fairies, and do nothing but dance and sing, and I shall allow them to go about on earth for twenty-four hours once a year and play their antics, but they shall do no mischief.'

'How long are the birds to remain in that state?' asked the king.

'I'll give them 2,000 years, your Majesty; and at the end of that time they are to go back into birds, as they were before. And after the birds change from the fairy state back into birds, they shall never breed more, but die a natural death.'

So the tribes lost their birds, and the King of Persia made such fearful havoc amongst them that they decided to leave the country.

They travelled, supporting themselves by robbery, until they came to a place where they built a city, and called it Troy, where they were besieged for a long time.

At length the besiegers built a large caravan, with a large man's head in front; the head was all gilded in gold. When the caravan was finished they put 150 of the best warriors inside, provided with food, and one of them had a trumpet. Then they pulled the caravan, which ran upon eight broad wheels, up to the gates of the city, and left it there, their army being drawn up in a valley near by. It was agreed that when the caravan got inside the gates the bugler should blow three loud blasts to warn the army, who would immediately advance into the city.

The men on the ramparts saw this curious caravan, and they began wondering what it was, and for two or three days they left it alone.

At last an old chieftain said:

'It must be their food.'

On the third day they opened the gates, and attaching ropes, began to haul it into the city; then the warriors leaped out, and the town was taken after great slaughter; but a number escaped with their wives and children, and fled on to the Crimea, whence they were driven by the Russians, so they marched away along the sea to Spain, and bearing up through France, they stopped. Some wanted to go across the sea, and some stayed in the heart of France; they were the Bretoons. The others came on over in boats, and landed in England, and they were the first people settled in Great Britain; they were the Welsh.

*　　*　　*　　*

JOHN JONES OF ANGLESEY

Amid the bare, rolling hills of Anglesey lived John Jones, a wealthy man and well connected.

From a boy John Jones had been short in stature, with a round, protuberant belly, like that of a mush-fed negro child; nor did this stoutness decrease with age, on the contrary, at forty John Jones could only just span his belly with both his hands—for his limbs, like his torso, were short and stout.

John Jones was a dark-haired, explosive Welshman, but not quite sharp; his neighbours who 'had English' called him 'rather soft', but that mattered little to him for he had much money, a fine house and a large garden; indeed, horticulture was his hobby, cock-fighting his serious occupation. He married young and was blessed with two daughters. Soon after marriage John Jones established an annual custom of showing his servants his wealth, the golden sovereigns tightly wedged into a stout, iron-bound, oaken chest, kept in a strong room. All his fortune was there, for in those days in remote rural districts everyone was his own banker. Upon such anniversary John Jones would throw open the lid and say cheerily to his assembled household—

'Now, my children, you can have all that you can take with your finger and thumb, but mind you don't use a knife,' and he chuckled, his fat sides shaking with laughter as the tender-nailed housemaid, Mary, tried without avail to extract a roll of sovereigns, so tightly were they packed. As no one else made an attempt, the lid of the great chest was shut down, bolted and padlocked, and the cheery John Jones returned to the kitchen, where to took a seat, cut a quid of twist and began to spit over the fireirons and fender, as was his habit. Mary, who was new to the house, placed a burnished spittoon near her master, who, noticing the attention, remarked—

'What's that for my girl? If you don't take that thing away I'll spit into it.'

'That's what it is for, master,' said Mary, demurely.

'Oh, indeed now, I thought it was kept too nice looking to dirty,' replied John Jones.

Soon after marriage, John Jones assumed the title of Captain, a rank as common in Wales as that of Colonel in the Western States, for everybody is a Captain in Wales, even unto the widows of old collier masters.

Well, Captain John Jones, as we shall hereafter call the subject of our memoir, was in need of a page to button his boots and go to the shop for his twist, so a smart lad of seven was found just suited to the work. Two weeks after this page entered into the service, his master called him by name, saying—

'Well, my boy, saddle the pony and go to Beaumaris and get me a lot of twist at William Williams.'

'Yes, master,' replied the page, and went on his errand. Upon his return the Captain took a long roll of twist with which he measured the lad from top to toe, cutting off what was over and handing the boy the piece which measured his height, saying—

'There, my boy, I wanted to see how much you had grown—there, take that, it's your share—away you go.'

So the lad soon learned to chew tobacco, a habit he never relinquished to the day of his death.

Soon after this episode the page ran away one day to attend a cock-fight at Llangefni. As it rained hard during his absence, Nellie, the cook, put the lad's coat in the yard on a hamper, and at eventide, before the boy returned, his master asked—

'Where's the boy?'

'Oh, master, he's dripping wet, just see his coat,' and Nellie produced the sobbing garment.

'Oh! bless you, Nellie, the boy will die, the boy will die. Give him something hot and send him to bed immediately.'

Nellie took the something hot and the young rascal escaped.

A few days after this ruse the Captain received a note from a neighbour, telling him there was a pair of valuable pigeons—

tumblers—for him if he would send over a messenger for them; whereupon the page was called and the Captain said—

'John, saddle the pony and go over to Llanfaes to Mr. Owen's and take a hamper, for you must fetch a pair or rare pigeons, and be sure, my boy, put a tally on their necks so you will know them again.'

When the boy returned the Captain, who met him in the drive, said—

'Well, boy, have you got them?'

'Yes, master.'

'Let me look at them now.'

'Oh, master, if you open the hamper, they'll fly away.'

'Not a bit of it boy; open the hamper at once.'

The hamper was opened, the pigeons escaped, wheeled, got their bearings and flew off towards Llanfaes.

'Good God, what a stupid fool I am to be sure, but they are sure to go home. Go back and fetch them,' said the Captain.

'Well, master, if I do I can't get back till tomorrow.'

'Why, boy?'

'Why, dear master, I can't catch them till they go to roost.'

'Well, to be sure, my boy; well, stay there and bring them tomorrow.'

So the boy got what he sought—leave to have a spree in the servants' hall at Llanfaes, for there was to be a jollification that night in honour of St. David. Indeed, he wore a leek in his cap on his return the next day with the rare and valuable pigeons, who were safely housed in a large box covered with wire netting. But the Captain never took much interest in them, he preferred his game-cocks—indeed, his greatest ambition was to win the first prize at the Llangefni Cock Fair, so that his delight knew no bounds when his friend at Llanfaes, a great amateur of pigeons and poultry, wrote and offered him a splendid game-cock.

As the page was riding away to fetch the prize, the Captain cried after him—

'Mind you make them put a tally on his neck and don't you let him out of your hands, boy.'

When the hamper arrived the Captain took it carefully into the tool-house and letting out the bird he examined it critically from comb to spur, muttering—

'Ah! he's a splendid bird, ah! he's a splendid bird,' then

turning to the page who stood by, he said, 'Now go and ask Jane if she has any red morocco.'

The lad returned and said Jane had plenty, whereupon the Captain replaced the cock in the hamper, fastened the lid, and waddled to Nellie in the kitchen and asked, 'Who will be the best sewer in the house, Nellie?'

'Well, indeed, I don't know, master, but I think it will be Mary.'

So the bonny Mary was called and ordered to sew a pair of red morocco leggings on to the game-cock, leaving his formidable spurs free. When he was duly buskined, he was turned loose among the other fowls.

'Now you see I'll be sure to know the bird,' said the Captain to his coachmen, 'he's a splendid bird, a splendid bird, he's sure to win at Llangefni.'

'Yes, indeed, sir, he looks it,' said the coachman, who was a connoisseur in these matters; indeed, the men servants of the establishment were as great cock-fighters as their master and they always clubbed in profit or loss.

As soon as the Captain had gone in, the coachman called his brother servants and showed them the cock, and this experienced trio soon decided that the handsome bird was good enough for the £20 prize at Llangefni Fair, so Mary, who was courting close with the footman, was bribed and the red leggings quickly transferred to another game-cock. The next morning immediately after breakfast the Captain went out and asked the coachman—

'How's the bird? How's the bird?'

'Oh! he's hopping about nicely, master.'

'Oh! there he is, look at his red buskins, that's him; isn't he a splendid bird?'

'Yes, indeed, master.'

'I'm sure to win the first prize with that.'

'Indeed, I hope so, sire,' and though the Captain had so poor an eye for the points of a good bird he thought himself a good judge, and yet any Spanish peasant would have a better idea of a *pize gallo*.

At length the great fair day came, three prizes being offered for the cock-fight—values £20, £10 and £5 each.

The Captain was there with his bird in a hamper and the servants were there with their bird and many another was there with his bird. Several fights were decided before the Captain's red-legged bird was matched against an old farmer's cock. The two birds sparred and soon began in good earnest, the farmer's bird winning, this success so exciting his owner that he jumped into the cock pit and trod accidentally on the Captain's bird's toes. The Captain was out of temper and he knocked the farmer down, after which there was much spitting and loud talking, when the Captain's butler went up behind the farmer and said quietly, 'Toot, carrots, you'll get something tonight, dry up!' and the farmer took the hint.

Cock-fight after cock-fight was decided until, amid loud cheering and noisy betting, the servants' bird was declared the winner of the great prize, at which the irate Captain turned upon the farmer and swore—

' 'Twas all that man's treading on his foot.'

'You struck me horrid and I am going to take the law of you,' retorted the farmer as he left the booth, whereupon the butler went up to his master and said,

'You did strike him horrid, sir, and he'll be sure to take the law.'

'Good God, where is he?' cried the Captain, whereupon the farmer was called.

'Well, Mr. Roberts, you see I'd have won the first prize only you trod on his foot; take care I don't catch you in the ring again. I know I've a hasty temper so here's £5 and forget the blow.'

And thus ended the cock-fight at Llangefni Fair.

That night the Captain was missing from home, his wife and children being away at the time. His devoted page immediately took the pony and scoured the country in search of his master, returning at ten o'clock in bright moonlight without having found a trace of him. Truth to tell, the Captain had walked home through a ravine with some soft places, his heavy body sinking up to his armpits. After struggling violently for several minutes, to his horror he saw the banshee or will o' the wisp hovering over the bog and laughing at him. Being a superstitious man he bellowed for help, and still the banshee danced and laughed at him. Fortunately his cries were heard by two farmers who were driving home along the highway. When they found the poor Captain bogged they tried hard to pull him out, but in vain, so one sat down to keep him company, whilst his companion drove to the Captain's house for servants, planks and ropes. The whole establishment turned out, and when they arrived at the ravine and saw their master in doleful dumps they began giggling. The captain grew angry and turning to a farmer said—

'Don't you see they are laughing at me? Oh, the beggars! If I had them in a room I would horsewhip them one and all, girls and all. They are laughing just like the banshee; it was a woman banshee. Oh, oh!'

His servants, with suppressed laughter, pulled his huge bemired carcase on the the ground—when he began to swear and they to laugh.

'Toot,' said the Captain solemnly, 'my own servant laughing at me, the same as that horrid banshee!' and then growing excited he shouted—

'Every one of you will leave the house tomorrow, every one! What, you laughing too, Nellie!'

'Oh, dear master,' said the favourite, 'you look like a ghost and you are such a sight we can't help laughing.'

'Well, I must give in if I look like that,' said the poor Captain meekly, and the party returned to the house.

*   *   *   *

THE PELLINGS

In a meadow belonging to Ystrad, bounded by the river which falls from Cwellyn Lake, they say the fairies used to assemble, and dance in fair moonlight nights. One evening a young man, who was the heir and occupier of this farm, hid himself in a thicket close to the spot where they used to gambol. Presently they appeared, and when in their merry mood, out he bounced from his covert, and seized one of their families; the rest of the company dispersed themselves, and disappeared in an instant. Disregarding her struggling and screams, he hauled her to his home, where he treated her so very kindly that she became contented to live with him as his maid-servant; but he could not prevail upon her to tell him her name.

Some time after, happening again to see the fairies upon the same spot, he heard one of them saying, 'The last time we met here our sister Penelope was snatched away from us by one of the mortals.' Rejoiced at knowing the name of his *incognita*, he returned home; and as she was very beautiful and extremely active, he proposed to marry her, which she would not for a long time consent to; at last, however, she complied, but on this condition. 'That if ever he should strike her with iron, she would leave him, and never return to him again.'

They lived happy for many years together, and he had by her a son and daughter; and by her industry and prudent management as a housewife he became one of the richest men in the country. He farmed, besides his own freehold, all the lands on the north side of Nant-y-Bettwys to the top of Snowdon, and all Cwm Brwynog in Llanberis, an extent of about 500 acres or upwards.

Unfortunately, one day Penelope followed her husband into the field to catch a horse, and he, being in a rage at the animal as he ran away from him, threw at him the bridle that was in his hand, which unluckily fell on poor Penelope. She disappeared in an instant, and he never saw her afterwards, but heard her voice in the window of his room one night after, requesting him to take care of the children, in these words :

> Rhag bod anwyd ar fy mab,
> Tn rhodd rhowch arno gob ei dad;
> Rhag bod anwyd an liw'r cann,
> Rhoddwch arni bais ei mam.

That is :—

> Oh ! lest my son should suffer cold,
> Him in his father's coat unfold;
> Lest cold should seize my darling fair,
> For her, her mother's robe prepare.

These children and their descendants, they say, were called Pellings, a word corrupted from their mother's name Penelope, and Pellings is a surname found in North Wales to-day.

* * * *

THE LEGEND OF PENMON HOUSE

Penmon House (on the eastern tip of Anglesey, facing Puffin Island) was a lonely old stone house roofed with slate, standing in a deserted garden, whence you could see Black Point, Puffin Island and the sea beyond, while on the right frowning Orme's Head and the Menai Strait glittered in the sunlight at high water, whilst at low water the Dutchman's Bank lay

Geometry in industry . . . patterns made by cranes and derricks as Wylfa nuclear power station takes shape on its bed of rock.

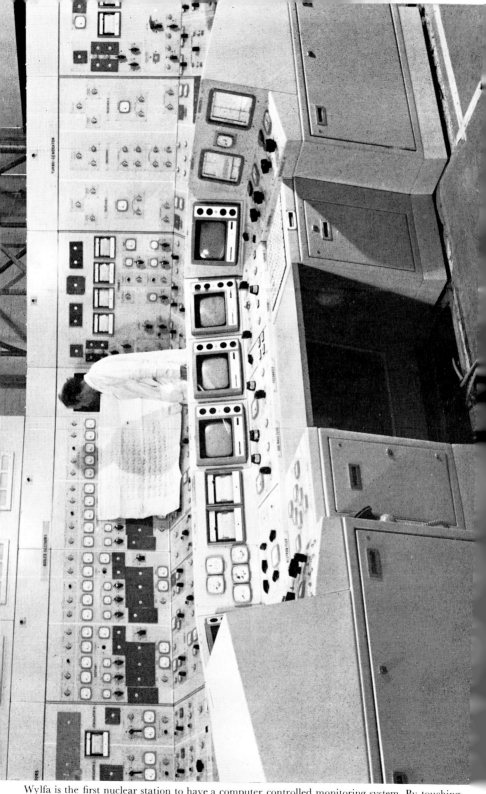

Wylfa is the first nuclear station to have a computer controlled monitoring system. By touching a button the staff can have a 24-hour state-report on 4,000 points all round the station.

exposed—a long sweep of sands.

Penmon House was a very old structure and had for long been unoccupied, the last inhabitants having been a man, his wife and daughter, strangers who came from nobody knew where and lived an exclusive life, spoke to none, and suddenly disappeared, the owner of the house never coming to search for them. Indeed, very little was known of the owner. It was said vaguely that he lived in Liverpool.

Not far from Penmon House was a little croft where an old fisherman lived, a curious old man with flowing white hair and long beard—Daddy Granby by name. He farmed his little croft, living all alone and minding his own business. Still, he was a matter of frequent discussion at the little beer house, nestling at the edge of the cliff, where he was often overhauled by the quarrymen as they drank their porter and sung 'lili-y lou bravi bron' to the music of fiddle and accordion; and splendid singers they were, those quarrymen, with their musical language and feeling. However, try as they might, they could never pick acquaintance with old Daddy Granby, and he lived out his life a mystery to the frequenters of the 'Pontydon'. But Owen Williams, the landlord of the inn, might have told something.

Daddy Granby lived in the old days when spirits and tobacco went on to the Isle of Man duty free. The people of Anglesey were sorely tempted to smuggle, and many a quiet Welsh fisherman made his pile in the contraband trade. Amongst these contrabandists was this same Owen Williams, who owned a smack, the King Llewelyn, in which his sons fished as a blind and smuggled for a living. Their practice was to anchor off Penmon Point, where a milk cart met them, for Penmon was a wild and lonely spot in those days, not even a lighthouse stood there to warn mariners off the rocks. But I must tell you of the milk cart, for this milk cart was of peculiar construction; it was simply a tank on wheels, the tank resting in a wooden casing which looked like a cart with two seats before and two seats behind. This cart belonged to an hotel in Beaumaris, and used to go back and forward to Daddy Granby's at Penmon for milk and often for spirits, for the two milk cans always carried in front were as often full of spirits as milk, for the casual observer could not tell the real and spirituous milk cans apart, but they were different—the spirituous cans being fitted with a pipe down the middle leading to the tap. That pipe alone was filled with milk, in case of an emergency. The smugglers always filled the tank full, so the spirit should not gurgle and slap about when driving over the hills to Beaumaris. So altogether there were six in the secret and they kept the business very close. The six were old Daddy Granby, the three Williamses, the innkeeper at Beaumaris and his brother—ostler and milk-cart driver.

When the sons had been for some years at the work, an artist, a middle-aged, dark-haired man, appeared at the 'Pontydon' and took up permanent quarters there, keeping a yacht moored off the shore, for he was very fond of sailing up and down the Strait as far as Menai, painting the islands, wooded shores and villages from his yacht. Especially fond was he of the two best views to be found in the Strait—Bangor from near Beaumaris, with Penrhyn Castle, and the view from Menai looking up the Strait on a fine summer's day. He painted these two lovely landscapes under different atmospheric effects, being especially fond of swiftly putting down evening and night effects of Bangor as seen from his yacht when moored off Beaumaris— and lovely is the scene when the lights twinkle through a light mist.

During his wanderings up and down the Strait he fell in with the Williamses and got very friendly, for Mr. George Harris, a Cornishman, was a good fellow. By degrees old Owen let him in to the secret of the smuggling, and Mr. Harris being of a romantic nature begged to be taken on some of those risky voyages to the Man. Owen and his sons trusted and took him, so that when Daddy Granby died two years after Mr. Harris' coming to the inn he was quite friendly with the Williamses, and full of sympathy for their great loss sustained by the death of their confederate, Daddy Granby, for the croft was let to a stranger, which was a bad look-out for their smuggling.

Soon after Daddy Granby's death, the news went round the village that an old man had hired old Penmon House and gone their to live, and that Mr. Harris had left, having sold his yacht for a song to the three Williamses. It was also remarked old Owen must be getting rich as he kept on the smack in addition to the yacht.

When the quarrymen and rustics had imbided these pieces of news, they settled down to sing, only regretting Mr. Harris' departure, for he was very free-handed with beer.

It was a Tuesday night in the following October, when all the usual frequenters of the 'Pontydon' were assembling, when Robert Roberts, a slate cutter, burst into the room, breathing hard, his face white as a sheet and his dark eyes staring wildly about him, saying excitedly, 'The ghost, the ghost!' and dropped into a seat.

There was a hobble-bobble amongst the quarrymen, for they are very superstitious—the Welsh. And when Robert Roberts got composed he told them he was coming down the lane, a steep bit of road, when he saw a hearse and four horses coming up from the sea, and he drew back and saw them go by. 'They came up rightly slow. There were four horses with white heads and white fore-legs, white as a sheet, and two postillions all dressed in white on the fore-horses, and their faces burning like fire, and then came a hearse, all the wheels burning like fire, and behind was a big ghost, about eight feet high, with a glassy face, all burning like fire, and they went by and never made no noise at all.'

The quarrymen looked at each other and kept questioning poor Robert Roberts, so that there was no music that night, and they went in a body to the village—to find all their doors locked and the women in terror for a ghost; a big tall man all in white, with a face like fire, had been walking through the village that evening.

The inhabitants of the village had a sleepless time that watch, and for many a night afterwards, for many saw the ghostly hearse and tall spirit with the flaming face. The hearse always drove to old Penmon House and was never seen only between the sea and the old house, so that Penmon House soon got the reputation of being haunted, and no one ever went near it. But the old hermit did not seem to mind, though like Daddy Granby he would speak to no one.

XI

ISLAND GAZETTEER

SAILING THE COAST

Without in any sense forgetting the beauty and the peace of the interior of the island of Anglesey—including the area formerly known as 'Little Anglesey' to which reference is made later in this chapter—the coastline is among the most romantic and colourful in Britain. Sailing activities are centred on Beaumaris—with the headquarters of the Royal Anglesey Yacht Club and an annual regatta in the Menai Strait —and at Holyhead, Trearddur Bay, Red Wharf Bay, Bull Bay and Cemaes Bay.

Sailing the coastline—armed with charts and pilot book —can be a rewarding way of discovering Anglesey. For this purpose the coastline can be divided into sections (as in F. H. Glazebrook's *'Anglesey and the North Wales Coast'*) and the extracts which follow (since this is not a guide-book) will, I hope, at least help the stranger in Anglesey to find his way about.

THE MENAI STRAIT

BEAUMARIS itself, looking across to the mountains of Caernarvonshire, is the key to the north-eastern section of the Strait, running from Penmaenmawr to Carnarvon Bar. This ancient county town of Anglesey (the Cowes of the North, it has been called) with its beautiful, broad expanse of water, was built—its castle, too—by Edward I in 1295, taking three thousand men three years to do. The town walls are a later addition, built in the fifteenth century to combat the Glendower Rising.

Beaumaris was originally known as Porth Wygyr, a Viking name suggesting it was known to the raiders from across the North Sea ten centuries ago. Edward I chose the French words beau marais—beautiful marsh. In this castle here King Edward is said to have held a fine banquet to which he invited many Welsh bards . . . and murdered them all.

Under the Tudors, Beaumaris flourished as a port, and its merchants grew rich. In the 18th and 19th centuries shipbuilding added to the town's reputation and wealth, vessels being built chiefly for the copper trade at Parys Mountain and for the slate industry at Penrhyn Quarry, near Bethesda on the mainland. Such Beaumaris built vessels as the Amlwch, seventy-six tons, built in 1786, and the Warren Bulkeley, a sloop of seventy-seven tons, built in 1803, carried many cargoes of Anglesey copper and Caernarvon slate to London. Today, a yacht builder's yard upholds a tradition going back to the Middle Ages.

The Bull's Head (1472) is one of the interesting inns of Beaumaris. It was commandeered by General Mytton, Cromwell's general, while he besieged the castle in 1645 and it was here that Charles Dickens and Dr. Johnson stayed and drank their ale while visiting the town. Still working properly today at the Bull is a water clock by B. WORRELL 'of ye olde towne Exeter, A.D. 1695' showing a Death's Head and the words 'Tyme Wanes . . . Deth Claimes'.

The 14th century St. Mary's church was built when Beaumaris was an English settlement, and is more representative of English architecture than any other in Anglesey. The south porch contains the coffin of Princess Joan, daughter of King John, and wife of Llewelyn the Great. The coffin was discovered in a local farmyard, after being lost for several hundred years.

Near the church stands the Old Gaol built in the 19th century and containing one of very few tread-mills remaining in Britain. One of the last men to be hanged there protested his innocence to the end and just before the fateful moment he placed a curse on the church clock, saying that it would never be right from that day on. Even nowadays, one side of the clock tells a different time from the other and all attempts to rectify this have failed.

An old custom still carried out in the town is the hot coppers' ceremony of the Anglesey Hunt, in which a lady patroness of the hunt scatters hot coppers from the balcony of the Bulkeley Arms Hotel (Beaumaris has been linked with the Bulkeley family for more than five hundred years. William Bulkeley was Constable of the castle in 1440, as was a favourite of Elizabeth I, Sir Richard Bulkeley. The present Lord-Lieutenant of Anglesey is Sir Richard Williams-Bulkeley.)

Today the story of Beaumaris is being avidly followed as far away as Australia, where the Melbourne suburb of Beaumaris has formed a link with the 'mother' town strengthened, incidentally, by a visit to her Melbourne home a short while ago by Miss Eileen Owen, a receptionist at the Bulkeley Arms Hotel, who took with her greetings from Anglesey.

GARTH FERRY The earliest recorded ferry crossing the Menai Strait from Bangor was that of Porth Esgob, the 'Bishop's Crossing', which, from the 13th century to the middle of the 19th, plied between Gored-y-Gyt (below Upper Bangor) and Cadnant Creek and between Garth and Gallows Point. The old causeway, visible at low water to south-westward of Bangor Pier, was in use until 1857. The history of Bangor, on the mainland, centres around the early monastic settlement and later cathedral of Saint Deiniol, and from which the city received its name ban, high or celebrated, and cor, the choir part of a church. An older name for the town was y Cae On, the Ash Enclosure.

LLANDISILIO. The parish church of St. Tysilio stands on an islet in the Strait itself. Money from the sale of a short history of the parish written by Mr. David Senogles—he was born at Llandisilio and is now Chief Financial Officer of Beaumaris—goes to the maintenance of Church Island.

Tysilio was the son of Brochwel, a prince of Powys, and commander of the British forces defeated by Ethelfrid of Northumbria at the Battle of Chester in A.D. 603. Mr. Senogles tells us that Tysilio became a monk at Meifod, in Montgomeryshire, and some time between the years 590 and 600, established his sanctuary on the site of the present parish church on the little island in the Menai Strait.

Tysilio returned to Meifod as abbot and then moved on to a monastery near St. Malo, in Britanny, where he is buried.

PORT DINORWIC, or Felinheli (saltwater-mill) is—like Port Penrhyn also on the mainland, the other side of Bangor—a slate port. North Wales slate is the finest in the world, and the slates from the Dinorwic Quarries and the Penrhyn Quarries have been shipped to very many countries. Slate quarrying in Caernarvonshire went on in Elizabethan times, but it was not until the 18th century that the quarrying industry was placed on a commercial basis.

Dinorwic, or -wyg, a name suggesting Scandinavian origin,

refers to the early fortified camp or signal station situated on the small headland closing the southern end of the beach at Port Dinorwic. It may have been a military post in Roman times.

The shores of Menai to southward of Port Dinorwic are believed to have been the scene of the invasion of Anglesey by the Romans under Suetonius Paulinus in A.D. 61, and again in A.D. 76, under Julius Agricola. It is claimed that the Romans crossed the strait from Llanfair-is-Gaer (hence the name the Church of Saint Mary below the Camp) to a point under Llandidan called Pant-yr-Ysgraphie, the Inlet of the Ferryboats (a ferry service was run intermittently from the 13th to the 15th centuries).

ABER MENAI FERRY. This ferry—referred to as early as 1296—used to do a thriving business taking travellers across the Strait from Morfa Dinlle to Anglesey, and the country people from Newborough and elsewhere on the island to 'the big town' (Caernarvon) on market days. The point from which the ferry plied was known as Abermeney and later Southcrook—from the shape of the long peninsular of sand forming the southern extremity of Anglesey. On 5 December 1785 the ferryboat capsized with a shipload of passengers homeward bound from Caernarvon market and fifty people were drowned.

BELAN FORT was erected to command the narrow southern entrance to the Menai Strait by the first Baron Newborough when only the strength of the British Navy saved the country from invasion by the then all-victorious Napoleon Bonaparte at the close of the 18th century. Over a hundred years later Fort Belan was fortified again; and the sentry on the rampart again kept his vigil—this time for Hitler's sea and air forces.

THE WEST COAST

For many centuries the coastline from Llanfwrog to Llanrhyddlad, and from Trearddur Bay southwards to Rhoscolyn, Rhosneigr, and Aberffraw, was the favourite locality for wreckers and pirates, and Cymyran Beach, Traffwll Lake, Tafarn y Cwch (The Boat Inn), and Cymunod are inseparably associated with a fascinating, elusive and mysterious 'White Lady' in the Percy Blakeney tradition.

In the centre of the beautiful stretch of coastline and on the western side of Holy Island is Trearddur Bay, a good anchorage in off-shore winds. Anchorages giving some degree of shelter in all weather may be found in many of the surrounding bays hidden away among the rocks.

HOLY ISLAND itself—one of many so named around the coasts of Britain—is joined to the main island by two bridges. Holyhead harbour is formed by one of the finest stone breakwaters anywhere along the British coastline, constructed on a foundation of many thousands of tons of stone quarried from the Holyhead Mountain (Mynydd Twr) and dumped into the sea. A metal plate on the wall at the far end of the breakwater records that work began in 1845 and that on August 19th, 1873, Albert Edward, Prince of Wales, declared the harbour complete.

The mountain top on Holy Island is only 720 feet above sea level but from it can be seen the whole wonderful vista of Snowdonia in one direction and, in the other, the Mountains of Mourne and the Wicklow Hills beyond the Irish Sea. Down below is the South Stack with its lighthouse built on a tiny island at the foot of high cliffs. For the ornithologist few places are more rewarding if he wishes to see a collection of sea-birds.

The cliffs near Holyhead, a few hundred feet high and falling sheer into the sea, have recently been 'discovered' by mountaineers. They formed the subject of a dramatic B.B.C. television broadcast showing a new climb of these rocks in 1966 by a party led by Christopher Bonington, one of Britain's outstanding climbers; a party which also included Tom Patey, the Scottish doctor who has climbed in the Himalayas, and the American expert Royal Robbins. To get to sea level on these cliffs involves a spectacular slide down the rope, after which comes the problem of finding a way up! It is a highly dangerous climb, the vertical rock face having a tendency to fall apart, and below the climber as he hangs, claws and twists on the rock face is nothing—nothing, that is, except the sea, cunningly lapping over hidden, jagged rocks which so easily can become a mountaineer's grave.

Of great interest to the antiquarian is a large group of circular hut dwellings on the side of Holyhead Mountain (the 'Huts of the Irish holy men'), dating from the 3rd and 4th centuries, whilst on the top is a hill fort called Caer y Twr, the Twr stronghold.

At the other end of Holy Island, in the south-west is Rhoscolyn, famed for its exceptionally equable climate even for Anglesey. It is an excellent place for fishing from boat or rock, shrimping and prawning. The cliffs are rich in wild flowers. From the quarry at Rhoscolyn marble was exported to many parts, and some may be seen in Bristol, Worcester and Peterborough cathedrals.

Saint Gwenfaen's Well, an early Christian holy well, is on the westward slope of Rhoscolyn Head, inland from the cliffs of Porth-y-Gwalch (Cove the Hawk). Its waters are said to have possessed, among other charms, the power of curing mental disorders—two white spars stones formed the necessary offering, and the answer was to be inferred from the manner in which bubbles appeared on the surface of the water.

One of Anglesey's great sea-faring characters of all time lived at Rhoscolyn—Hugh Hughes. Before he became coxswain for twenty-four years of the Rhoscolyn lifeboat, Hughes wrote this unemotional log of rescue work in his own fishing boat and with only the help of a few other fishermen :

1866   *In Cymeran Bay, with our own boat, saved from a full-rigged English ship twenty-four lives; the vessel a total wreck.*

1867   *In Rhosneigr Bay, with our own boats, saved from a Newfoundland brig ten lives; out from 10.30 p.m. till 2.00 a.m. A total wreck.*

1870   *In Cymeran Bay, sea too heavy for our boat to go out, saved with ropes eight men out of the crew of sixteen of a Spanish barque; a total wreck.*

1870   *In Porth Garren, with our own boat, picked up five men on floating spars belonging to a Spanish barque; a total wreck.*

1870   *In Rhoscolyn Bay, saved with ropes ten men from a three-masted English schooner.*

1874   *In Rhoscolyn Bay, saved with our own boat ten lives from a Newfoundland schooner; a total wreck.*

1875   *In Cymeran Bay, with our own boats, twenty foot and twenty-six foot keel, saved twenty lives from a full-rigged Spanish ship; a total wreck.*

1881   *In Cymeran Bay, saved with our own boat fifteen lives from an English barque; a total wreck.*

Total number of lives saved: 102.

RHOSNEIGR has grown in the last few years from a remote fishing village to a charming little town, still unspoilt and uncommercialised, a place to which the same families of business people—mainly from the Midlands of England—have been taking their children for two and three generations to enjoy its vast, open sands and glorious sunsets over the sea westwards to Ireland. Its name may come from Rhos-yn-Eigyr—the Moor of the Maid—although a less romantic suggestion is that the original name was Rhos-y-Neidr, meaning Moor of the Adder.

The early history of Rhosneigr centres on the valley of the little Afon Crigyll, the haunt of man since prehistoric times. Near the left bank of this stream are the remains of two cromlechau, those of Pentre Traeth and Ty Newydd, while the remains of a third and similar monument can be seen on the headland of Pen-y-Cnwc on the north side of Cable Bay. This is called Barclodiad-y-Gawres (the Giantess's Apronful) referring to the heap of stones forming the cromlech which has been reconstructed by the Ministry of Works and is today one of the most impressive cromlechs in Wales.

Coast erosion has enlarged Rhosneigr Bay and the Crigyll must once have been a navigable river entering the sea about a mile beyond the present coastline. In the early Middle Ages it was the scene of raids by Irish and Scandinavian rovers, and in later years it was associated with piracy around Rhosneigr. It was here that the Grigyll Robbers lured ships to destruction and hid the spoils in the sandhills. An official record of the County Gaol, Beaumaris, reads 'On Tuesday, April 25, 1715, was committed for felony, three men, known as the Lladron Creigiau Crigyll, who were found guilty of plundering the wreck of the sloop called The Charming Jenny, stranded at Crigyll'.

Southwards from Rhosneigr miles of lonely, sandy coves stretch away—many difficult to get at except by boat from the sea, but ideal for those seeking peace and quietude.

At the south-western tip of Anglesey, on one side of Malltraeth Bay, is the fascinating LLANDDWYN ISLAND (see Chapter Five) and on the other the former royal village of

ABERFFRAW, capital of North Wales from the time of Rhoderic the Great in 870 to that of the last Llewellyn in 1282.

Here, too, at Aberffraw, where the noise of so many battles against invaders from across the sea resounded so often, is the setting of the wedding of Bronwen. This story of Celtic mythology from the *Mabinogion* tells how Bronwen, daughter of Llyr, was at Harlech at the court of her brother Bendigeid Vran, King of Britain; how Matholwch, King of Ireland, came to ask for her hand in marriage; how a great wedding feast was held at Aberffraw; and how a wretched brother of the bride's, Evnissyen, angered and insulted Matholwch by shamefully maltreating his horses out of sheer pique at not being consulted about the wedding. It tells of Bronwen's adventures in Ireland, of her popularity, of the jealous scheming of her husband's relations, which eventually brought about an invasion of Ireland by Bendigeid Fran. The story ends, as far as concerns Anglesey, with the flight of Bronwen accompanied by the seven survivors of the disastrous campaign, bearing with them the head of Bendigeid Fran.

THE NORTH COAST

This section takes in the remainder of the Anglesey coastline, in a sweeping arc all the way from the Skerries Rock, off the north-west tip of the island, to Puffin Island off the eastern coast above Beaumaris, an area of colour and character similar in many ways to the coast of Britanny.

SKERRIES ROCK. For more than two hundred years there has been a warning light on Skerries Rock, from the time when a fire of coals burning in a brazier threw its glow over the sea, to the erection of a modern, four million candle-power lighthouse. The history of the Skerries light shows the founder of the lighthouse to have been William Trench, an Irish man, born in 1642, who obtained a ninety-nine years lease of the Skerries from William Robinson of Gwersyllt and Mynachdy at a rent of ten pounds a year until a beacon was built and 'thereafter a rent of twenty pounds per annum'. In the following year Trench was granted a patent by Queen Anne which empowered him to erect a beacon on the Skerries and to levy dues of 'one penny per ton upon all shipping benefiting by the light except our ships of war'.

On 4 November 1716 a light was first exhibited on the Skerries. By 1725 William Trench had died and the lighthouse passed into the possession of his widow's son-in-law, the Rev. Sutton Morgan. Five years later by Act of Parliament Morgan was given power to enforce payment of proper dues, but he died before being able to benefit from his new powers. His interest in the Skerries passed to his niece, Rebecca Morgan, the light dues by this time amounting to the comparatively large sum of £1,100 a year.

Ownership continued to change, and by 1839 Trinity House offered Morgan Jones £300,000, but the owner refused to sell what was the next year to become the only private lighthouse left. Finally, in 1841 a special jury sitting at the Sheriff's Court in Beaumaris decided that Trinity House should acquire this small, seaweed-covered piece of rock at a price of nearly £500,000.

DINAS GYNFOR is the site of an early British cliff fortress, one of the largest in Anglesey, and Gynfor was probably the name of the chieftain who erected these defences. Alternatively the name may be derived from a descriptive word meaning 'cut as with a chisel', which describes the sheer and narrow inlet on the eastern side of the headland called Porth Gynfor. Mining for china clay rocks to make porcelain, and brick works at nearby Porth Wen, have left some scars yet—strangely enough—the mellowed ruins have become an acceptable part of this beautiful part of The Highlands of Anglesey.

AMLWCH, a split in the rocky coast, was enlarged in 1793 to cope with the busy trade in the export of copper from Parys Mountain (see chapter nine). By 1785 the mines were already supplying the navies of Britain, France, Holland and Spain with copper bolts, nails and sheathing, and merchant ship-building concerns like the East India Company were big customers. The mines themselves were consuming 1000 tons of coal a day, most of which had to be imported. Forty vessels were engaged in the copper boom, and a local coinage—a penny piece—was struck in copper of a value equal to their purchasing power.

POINT LYNAS is on a stretch of majestic, rocky coast

with deep caves. Rock fishing is a rewarding pastime, and in one of the coves known as Safn Ci (Dog's Mouth) is Ffynnon Eilian—a well whose water is said to have health-giving properties, like that of the water at Ffynnon Ychen—an ever full cleft in the rocks near the church of Llaneilian, east of Amlwch.

The 18th and early 19th centuries saw a tremendous increase in the trade of the Port of Liverpool, and merchants and shipowners of the port, wanting to obtain early news of the arrival of their ships found the answer in a chain of semaphone stations, put up at high points along the coast of North Wales, and a series of flag poles from which the house flags of the ships sighted would be flown. Among these semaphone stations—the remains of which, including the substantial houses built by the Trustees of Liverpool Docks for the signalmen and their families, are still standing in several places—were those at Holyhead Mountain, above Port Lynas and on the tip of Puffin Island.

The men in charge of these stations became such expert signallers that a shipowner in Liverpool would often receive the information that his vessel was off Holyhead in less than a minute from the time of her number being ascertained, while the speed of transmission was such that the first part of the message would reach Liverpool before the last part had left Holyhead. In a special test of the efficiency of this semaphone system held in 1830 a message was sent out from Liverpool to Holyhead, and a reply received back in Liverpool, in twenty-three seconds. From 1860 onwards the old semaphone system was gradually superseded by electrical transmission.

Sailing coastwise round the north of Anglesey there is a familiar sight—the Liverpol Pilot Cutter, flying her red and white flag. Year in and year out, in all weather, the pilot cutter will be seen standing by somewhere near Point Lynas, to launch her boarding punt and put the Liverpol Pilot aboard a cargo ship.

In bad weather a high degree of seamanship is shown in getting these pilots aboard the ships, and typical of this skill is the occasion in 1881 when north-west gales had blown hard for several days and twelve sailing ships, awaiting pilotage in Liverpool Bay, were in danger of being ashore. The cutters found it impossible, because of the huge waves at the entrance to the Mersey, to put pilots aboard these twelve vessels, and the commander of No. 2 Pilot Cutter then decided to signal the sailing ships to 'follow the leader'. Setting his course straight for the channel, he led all ships into port.

DULAS. The old name for Ynys Dulas was Ynys Gadarn, from *cadarn* meaning strong. Ynys-y-Gadarn, or KEDEYRN, Isle of the Mighty, was an old Welsh name for Britain. Here, about half a mile from City Dulas, is a granite celtic cross commemorating the brothers Morris of Welsh literary fame who, sons of a cooper and carpenter, lived at a farm called Pentre Eirianell in the parish of Llanfihangel Tre'r Beirdd. A stone tablet at the roadside stile above the Pilot Boat Inn has an inscription relating to the memorial.

Dulas and the nearby Lligwy Bay are examples of places where the sailing explorer of Anglesey must go ashore and climb inland on foot—up to, for example, Mynydd Bodafon, a 500 ft. hill set aside a stretch of rugged country—a Lake District in miniature. From Mynydd Bodafon the view is superb—small freshwater tarns encircled by the moors and the landscape dotted with the typical white and colour-washed cottages of Anglesey wrapped around by patchwork carpets of gorse and heather—if there are Welsh fairy folk this, surely, is their home.

Even the 'mountain' itself is unique, its rocks being composed of a quartzite older than the oldest sections of the pre-Cambrian Mona Complex. On the western side of the hill is the site of Tre-'r-beirdd, a centre of druidical culture. The site of a pre-historic village of hut circles, or Cytiau-r'-Gwyddelod, is on the south-east side, and on the summit itself was an ancient signal station where beacons gave warning of the approach of invaders.

At Lligwy itself is one of the finest examples of a megalithie tomb in the country, with its entrance facing east—thus again supporting the theory that the people who built this cromlech and similar circles were sun worshippers. In connection with Lligwy cromlech there is a local tradition that a fisherman, seeking shelter in the cromlech from a storm, fell asleep and dreamed that someone was struggling in the water of Lligwy Bay and crying for his help. The fisherman went down to the sea, and there he saw a strange woman struggling to reach land. The fisherman brought her safely to the shore and saw that she was a lovely maiden dressed in a white robe and wearing jewelled bracelets. Her first request was for the fisherman to carry her up to the 'great stone', and this he did.

'Ha, Ha!' cried the maiden when she had been set down by the cromlech. 'If I had been an ugly old hag, dressed in rags, you would have let me drown. I am a witch. I was in a ship in Lligwy Bay and cruel hands threw me overboard. When I saw you were my sole chance of life. I disguised myself, and here I am. But fear not', went on the witch, 'one good turn deserves another'. And in the palm of her hand she held out a little golden ball. 'See!' she cried, 'I give you this golden ball which contains a snake-skin charm. So long as you keep it safely, and allow no one to find it, good fortune will go with you. Once each year you must take the golden ball, with the snake-skin inside it, go down to the rocks and dip it in the sea. Then you must return it to its secret hiding place. Should you lose it, or part with it, or take the snake-skin out of it, then your good luck will be gone for ever'.

With these words the lovely maiden ran down to the sea jumped into a strange vessel—and sailed away.

For a while all went well and the fisherman prospered as he had never done before. But one day, when he was dipping the golden ball in the sea as he had been told to do, he was tempted to take it out with him in his fishing boat to help bring him a record catch of fish. But somehow the ball fell in the sea and was lost.

At once the fisherman's luck began to turn, and for weeks the wretched man spent his days wandering along the shore looking for the golden ball. At last one day he found it in a pool at low tide, and taking it home he put it once more in its secret hiding place. Prosperity returned to him, and he and his children and his children's children lived happily ever after!

MOELFRE has always been 'in the news' of seafaring drama. Crews of the lifeboat have saved nearly 600 lives, and one of their most dramatic rescues was in October 1959 when —under their coxswain Richard Evans—they saved the crew of the 'Hindlea' in a gale of over 100 m.p.h. This was almost a century to the day when the Royal Charter sank in the bay on her return with gold diggers from Australia (see Chapter Six).

Another of the harrowing sea stories associated with Moelfre is that of the submarine Thetis which sank in Liverpool Bay in

June 1939 during a trial run, with the loss of ninety-nine men out of the 103 on board—believed due to the failure to close the cap of one of her torpedo tubes. It was to the little sandy bay of Traeth Bychan that this 'steel graveyard' was brought after she had been raised from the sea floor by slinging the vessel under the hull of a collier. The Thetis was repaired and, with the country at war by then, began an adventurous career as the Thunderbolt. Under the command of Lieut. Commander Bernard Crouch, D.S.O., she sank two U-Boats and five German supply ships until, in the spring of 1943, some unknown fate again overtook the submarine and the Admiralty announced that 'H.M.S. Thunderbolt is overdue and must be considered lost'. Once more this ship is a graveyard on the seabed—somewhere.

RED WHARF BAY. Quiet coves and fine sands are the feature of this wide bay, nearly three miles across at its mouth. On the north side of the bay is Castell-Mawr, a big limestone block resembling a castle and the site of an early British fortress. Across the bay is the village of Llanddona (with its B.B.C. television transmitting station for North Wales) and, very near the coastline, Bwrdd Arthur (Arthur's Table)—another early British hill fortress where parts of the original walls and the remains of hut circles can be seen.

At one time the district round Llanddona was known as 'the land of witches'. A famous witch was one Shani Bwt or Little Jane, who, at forty years of age, was only three feet eight inches in height, and had two thumbs on her left hand. The witches of Llanddona are believed to have been the descendants of survivors from a Spanish ship wrecked in Red Wharf Bay. Then men and women who reached the shore of the bay near Llanddona were allowed to remain and settle down in the neighbourhood. The story goes that some among them were able to perform certain conjuring tricks, and this, together with the fact that they were red-headed foreigners and therefore objects of suspicion, caused the superstitious inhabitants of the district to believe that they were in league with the devil.

From Bwrdd Arthur on round the coast towards Puffin Island north-east of Beaumaris—a stretch described in one old account in these picturesque words : 'The shore is very rude, and terrific to navigators and many of its rock are fine and

Another aspect of modern Anglesey. A landing craft built by Anglesey craftsmen
undergoing trials off Beaumaris.

Open working at the Parys Mine, c. 1785, from a water colour by J. C. Ibbetson in 'Art and the Industrial Revolution'. (F. D. Klingender).

picturesque, rising to a great height. These craggy prominces afford shelter to that wily animal the fox, and the best dogs find great difficulty to unhouse him'.

PUFFIN ISLAND lies off the coast beyond the Penmon lighthouse, the home now only of seabirds—including the charming little Puffin from which its gets its present-day name —and, in the waters around, the playground of seals.

The island has had a variety of names, including Ynys Seiriol (Seiriol's Island) after Saint Seiriol landed there in the 6th century and built a sanctuary; Ynys Glanawg, after Glanawg the father of Helig, Prince of Morfa Rhianedd; Priest's Island (or Priestholme), the name given it by Vikings in the 10th century; and Ynys-y-Llygod, Island of Mice, from an old legend.

A 12th century historian writes of Puffin Island:

'There is a small island almost adjoining to Anglesey, which is inhabited by hermits, living by manual labour and serving God. It is remarkable that when, by the influence of human passions, any discord arises among them, all their provisions are devoured and infected by a species of small mice, with which the island abounds, but when the discord ceases they are no longer molested. Nor is it to be wondered at if the servants of God sometimes disagreed, for these are the temptations of human infirmity, yet virtue is often made perfect by infirmity, and faith is increased by tribulations. This island is called in Welsh, Ynys Lenach, or Priest's Island, because many bodies of saints are deposited there, and no woman is suffered to enter it.'

The only building now on Puffin Island, besides the ruined monastery of Saint Seiriol, is the old semaphone telegraph station.

'LITTLE ANGLESEY'

The area of the island formerly known by this name, and famed for its healthy air, runs across the whole breadth of the island, south of a line from Malltraeth to Red Wharf Bay and from Llanddwyn Island in the west to Puffin Island in the east. It has a considerable expanse of coastline on either side of the island and along the Menai Strait, with sheltered coves and sandy bays. Inland it has some of the best villages, set

I

among meadowland, marshes and heather-clad commons. For the naturalist the whole district is among the richest in rare plants, fossils, minerals and bird life.

On the 'top', or north-western side of 'Little Anglesey' is the county's administrative centre of Llangefni, a clean town of broad streets built on the edge of a shady, fern-covered glen called The Dingle. Being almost in the centre of the island, a journey from Llangefni to any part of the coast, or elsewhere in the interior, is easy and takes very little time. Into the town every week come farmers and traders from every part of Anglesey, making its weekly market one of the biggest and most colourful in all Wales and attended by some who can claim many generations of association with the event. Two farmhouses on the edge of Llangefni are part of Welsh history —Tregarnedd, the home of Ednyfed Fychan, counsellor of Llewelyn the Great; and Plas Penmyndd, home of Owen Tudor, grandfather of Henry VII, the first of the Tudor kings.

Appendix (i)

AN ISLAND MISCELLANY

For a holiday that is different,' says the Anglesey Tourist Association guidebook, 'COME TO ANGLESEY'. Here then, are some useful facts for the new visitor to this intriguing island :

CLIMATE

Equable; extremes of any kind are rare. The season is a fortnight earlier than on the mainland generally and the sunshine record is at places second only to Sidmouth, in South Devon. On the few occasions when snow falls in winter it rarely lies for more than three or four days. The county's annual rainfall is between thirty-five and forty inches, while temperatures average just over forty degrees in January and over sixty degrees in July.

COMMUNICATIONS

Anglesey is unique among the islands of Britain in having both a classic main railway line and a trunk highway linking it directly over its great road and rail bridges with the mainland and London itself, 250 miles from Llangefni. Passenger services by sea also link Anglesey with Ireland, but there is no civilian airport on the island.

The main railway line (the London and North-Western Railway—or 'Premier Line'—before the days of amalgamation and, later, British Rail) is the Euston to Holyhead via Chester route for the nightly steamships to Dun Laoghaire, in Ireland— and an extra day boat in the summer season. Before reaching Holyhead there are stations at Menai Bridge, Llanfairpwll, Bodorgan and Valley.

The fastest trains on the Euston to Holyhead run are the 'Irish Mail', 'Welshman' and 'Emerald Isle' expresses; the fastest time four and a half hours.

There are nine or more weekday trains from Holyhead to Bangor, calling in most cases at all stations, with a similar return service.

The road from London and the South is the A.5—Telford's Highway—and the island is linked with the North Country by the North Wales coastal roads A.55 and A.548 to Connah's Quay for Liverpol and further north, and for Chester and the North Midlands.

Buses run throughout Anglesey, and timetables are available from Crosville Motor Services' Traffic Department, Crane Wharf, Chester; or from local depots on the island.

Distance from Llangefni:

London 250 miles; Liverpool 90; Manchester 103; Rhyl 42; Colwyn Bay 28; Llandudno 28; Conway 23; Bangor 8; Caernarvon 17; Pwllheli 34; Criccieth 32; Llanberis 22; Amlwch 14; Holyhead 16; Menai Bridge 7; Beaumaris 9; Llanfair P.G. 5; Trearddur Bay 14; Rhosneigr 9; Benllech 6; Bull Bay 16; Red Wharf Bay 6; Malltraeth 6; Cable Bay 8.

INFORMATION OFFICES

WALES: The Welsh Tourist and Holidays Board (Bwrdd Croeso i Gymru) 7 Park Place, Cardiff.

ANGLESEY: The Anglesey Tourist Association, 27 High Street, Llangefni.

BANGOR: Librarian, Public Library.

LLANGEFNI: Council Offices, Llangefni.

NATIONAL TRUST: (Snowdonia National Park, Bodnant Gardens, Penrhyn Castle, etc.) H. J. D. Tetley, Dinas, Betws-y-Coed, North Wales).

SNOWDON RAILWAY: General Manager, Snowdon Mountain Railway, Llanberis, North Wales.

NEWSPAPERS

Herald Mon (Tuesday) and Holyhead and Anglesey Mail (Friday) published at Castle Square, Caernarvon; Holyhead Chronicle (Friday), North Wales Chronicle (Friday) and Y Clorianydd (Tuesday) published at Caxton House, Bangor; Y Cymro (Thursday) published at Caxton Press, Oswestry.

LIBRARIES

Anglesey County Library Service has branches at Llangefni, Holyhead, Amlwch, Beaumaris, Rhosneigr, Benllech, Cemaes, Newborough and Menai Bridge. Mobile library serves all remaining areas.

EDUCATION

County Secondary Schools: Sir Thomas Jones County Secondary School, Amlwch; David Hughes County Secondary School, Beaumaris; Holyhead County Secondary School; Llangefni County Secondary School.

Private Schools: Le Bon Sauveur, Holyhead; Trearddur House, Preparatory School for Boys.

The first centres in the United Kingdom to establish a comprehensive pattern of secondary education under the 1944 Education Act included Amlwch, Beaumaris, Holyhead and Llangefni. There is no eleven-plus examination in Anglesey, and the County Secondary School, Llangefni, has over nine hundred pupils all admitted without entrance examination.

COMMERCE

MARKETS: Llangefni (Thursday) and Holyhead (Saturday).

EARLY CLOSING: Tuesday at Holyhead and Llangefni. Wednesday at Amlwch, Beaumaris, Menai Bridge and Rhosneigr.

CUSTOMS & EXCISE: The Custom House is at Holyhead.

BANKS: Amlwch—Barclays, Midland, National Provincial; Beaumaris—Lloyds, Midland, National Provincial; Holyhead—Barclays, Lloyds, Midland, National Provincial, C.W.S.; Llangefni—Barclays, Lloyds, Midland, National Provincial; Menai Bridge—Midland, National Provincial; Rhosneigr—Midland, National Provincial. Sub-Offices in a number of villages.

HOSPITALS

King Edward Memorial Sanatorium and the Druid Hospital at Llangefni; Gors Maternity Hospital and Stanley Hospital at Holyhead; Caernarvonshire and Anglesey, at Bangor.

SPORT

BOWLS: There are two crown type bowling greens at Holyhead and others at Beaumaris, Llanfairpwll, Menai Bridge, Llangefni, Amlwch, Benllech and Trearddur Bay.

FOOTBALL: Most towns and villages have teams, many of which play in the Anglesey League.

GOLF: Holyhead Golf Club has an eighteen-hole course to the south of the town close to the southern shore of Holy Island. Beaumaris has the nine-hole Baron Hill Golf Club where visitors are welcome any day and a professional is in attendance. Bull Bay (Amlwch) Club has an eighteen-hole links on the cliff top; at Rhosneigr is the eighteen-hole links of the Anglesey Golf Club formed in 1914.

PUTTING: Greens at Beaumaris and Holyhead.

TENNIS: There are hard courts at Holyhead, Amlwch, Llangefni, Trearddur Bay, Menai Bridge, Benllech, and

Llanfairpwll. Grass Courts at Beaumaris.

RIDING SCHOOLS: Riding schools at Benllech, Dulas and Rhosneigr.

SAILING: Beaumaris is the headquarters of the Royal Anglesey Yacht Club who hold an annual regatta week in August. Sailing is also good at Holyhead, Trearddur Bay, Red Wharf Bay, Bull Bay, and Cemaes Bay.

CAMPING: Particulars of the many authorised camping and caravan sites may be obtained from the County Planning Officer, Anglesey County Council Offices, Llangefni.

WALKING: One of the best and most instructive of the walks for the naturalist in Anglesey is the Dingle, at Llangefni. Geologically it is rift in the normal trend of the island's central massif which follows the line of the Menai Strait. This rift deflects the River Cefni almost at right-angles to its would-be course before it again finds its normal line in the Malltreath Marsh. The Dingle provides, in a small compass, a remarkable range of scenery—pasture, ploughland, wooded slopes, and wild bogland—and similarly many species of bird life from warblers to various hawks.

COUNTY EVENTS

Anglesey County Eisteddfod—Whitsun weekend. County Agricultural Show, Llangefni—second week of August.

FISHING

Both freshwater game fishermen, and those who prefer the sea sport, find Anglesey a rewarding place to visit—some of the anglers seeking trout, for instance travel to Cefni Reservoir, at Llangefni, from all parts of England. In October 1966 a new reservoir was opened called Llyn Alaw. Fishing and boating are allowed. The sea offers ample flat fish, codlings, bass, cod, lobsters and pollock—the north and west coasts are excellent for rod fishing. In August and September sea trout enter most of the island's main rivers—the Alaw, Braint, Cefni, Ffraw and Wygyr, all of which contain brown trout.

There are two prerequisites to fishing in any waters:

1. A permit of the angling club, association, syndicate or estate in whose waters the angler intends to fish, or the permission of the fishery owner or occupier.
2. A licence issued by the Gwynedd River Board.

In Anglesey, the Gwynedd River Board's licence charges,

covering the whole of the island, are as follows :

			£	s.	d.
Salmon and/or Sea Trout	Season	...	4	0	0
Salmon and/or Sea Trout	Week	...	1	5	0
Salmon and/or Sea Trout	Day	...		10	0
Trout (excluding Sea Trout)	Season	...		15	0
Trout (excluding Sea Trout)	Week	...		10	0
Trout (excluding Sea Trout) Restricted to persons under the age of 16	Season	...		5	0

The board makes these points :

1. The River Board licence does not entitle the holder to fish in private waters without the permission of the owner or lessee.

2. The term 'salmon' includes 'trout'.

3. The term 'trout' includes 'char'.

4. The open seasons for fishing in the Gwynedd River Board are : salmon and sea trout—1st April to 17th October; trout (excluding sea trout)—1st March to 30th September.

Here are some of the places to fish :

Lake	Fish	
Lake Ffrogwy, Bodffordd	Trout Roach	
Wytheidion Lake, Cors Capel Coch, Llangefni	Trout Sea Trout	
Cadarn Lake, Llanbedrgoch	Rainbow Trout Trout	
Hendre Lake, Gwalchmai	Tench Roach	
Mynydd Bodafon Lake	Roach Perch	
Dorothea Lake, Mynydd Llwydiarth, Pentraeth	Trout Brown Trout	
Fodol Lake, Rhosgoch	Trout, fly fishing only; 14″ limit	£1 per day

Coron Lake,	Trout	
Bodorgan	Sea Trout	
Traffwil Lake	Roach	
	Perch	
	Trout	
Penrhyn Lake,	Perch	
Near Valley R.A.F.		
Dinas Road Lake,	Roach	
Near Valley R.A.F.		
Cefni Reservoir	Trout	Day 15/–
Maelog Lake,	Roach	
Rhosneigr	Trout	
	Perch	
Alaw Reservoir	Trout	Season £15
		Day £1
Alaw River,	Trout	
Llanfachraeth and	Sea Trout	
Llanddeusant		
River Wygyr,	Trout	Season £1
Cemaes	Fly fishing only	Day 2/6
	and limit 7″	
River Crigyll,	Trout	
Rhosneigr		

Appendix (ii)

A SELECT BIBLIOGRAPHY FOR
THE ANGLESEY READER

General

ANGLESEY COUNTY COUNCIL, County Development Plan. 2 vols. (1952)

EISTEDDFOD MON. Transactions.

ENDOWED CHARITIES OF ANGLESEY (1897)

EMERSON, P.H. Tales from Welsh Wales (1894). Also Welsh Fairy Tales and other Stories (1894).

EVANS, Lady G. Nesta. Religion and Politics in mid-eighteenth century Anglesey (1936).

EVANS, Lady G. Nesta. Social Life in mid-eighteenth century Anglesey (1936).

GRIFFITH, J. E. Pedigree of Anglesey (and Caernarvonshire) Families (1914).

HUGHES, D. LL. and WILLIAMS, D. Holyhead: the Story of a Port (1967).

LEWIS, Eiluned and Peter. The Land of Wales (1937).

LLOYD, D. M. & E. M. A book of Wales (1953).

LLWYD, Angharad. A history of the island of Mona (1833).

ROWLANDS, H. Mona Antiqua Restaurate : an archaeological discourse (in English) on the antiquities, natural and historical, of the Isle of Anglesey, the ancient seat of the British Druids (1723). A supplement to this volume—'Anon', but believed to be John Thomas (1775).

SKINNER. Ten days tour through Anglesey (1802).

TUNNICLIFFE, C. R. Shorelands Summer Diary (1952).

WILLIAMS, J. David Hughes and His Free Grammar School at Beaumaris (1933).

WILLIAMS, John (Beaumaris). History of Berw (1861).

(Note : Official booklet guides are available for Anglesey, Amlwch, Holyhead, Llangefni, and Penmon.)

Agriculture

ROBERTS, E. Great Britain Soil Survey. The County of Anglesey : soils and agriculture (1958).

Antiquities
ANGLESEY ANTIQUARIAN SOCIETY. Transactions 1913 to date.
CRASTER, O. E. Ancient Monuments of Anglesey. (Reprinted 1962.) (H.M.S.O. pamphlet guide)
FOX, Sir Cyril. A Find of the Early Iron Age from Llyn Cerrig Bach. (Anglesey, 1946.)
ROYAL COMMISSION ON ANCIENT AND HISTORICAL MONUMENTS, ANGLESEY. (1937, reprinted 1960.) H.M.S.O.
STANLEY, W. O. Antiquities in Holyhead Island (1871).
Communications
DUNN, J. M. The Chester and Holyhead Railway.
GLAZEBROOK, F. H. Anglesey and North Wales Coast (1962).
HARPER, Charles G. The Holyhead Road (1902).
WATSON, Edward. The Royal Mail to Ireland (1917).
Geology
GREENLY, Edward. Geology of Anglesey. 2 vols. (1927); and Memoir Geological Survey (1919).
Industry
ROWLANDS, J. Copper Mountain. A.A.S. (1966).
MANNING, W. The Parys and Mona Mines in Anglesey; the future of non-ferrous mining in Gt. Britain and Ireland. Institute of Mining and Metallurgy (1959).
Natural History
ANGLESEY ANTIQUARIAN SOCIETY (TRANSACTIONS 1913–1952, as follows :—)
Bird life on the coast of Anglesey (Glazebrook, 1926, 1928, 1929, 1931 and 1934).
Some birds of Anglesey (Bulkeley 1938).
Some sea-birds (Thomas, 1935).
An account of the littoral fauna of the Anglesey coast from the Menai Strait (Jackson, 1940).
Some account of the botanical exploration of Anglesey (Carter, 1952).
A note on Anglesey flora (Clegg, 1950).
Studies in the flora of Anglesey and Caernarvonshire lakes (Woodhead, 1939).
Newborough Warren—some notes on its wild life (Aspden, 1933).

A list of Anglesey lepidoptera (Baynes, 1913).

DAVIES, Hugh. Welsh Botanology—a Systematic Catalogue of the Native Plants of the Isle of Anglesey (1813).

GRIFFITH, J. E. Flora of Anglesey and Caernarvonshire (1932).

The Sea

DAVIES, H. R. A review of the records of the Conway and the Menai Ferries (1942).

ROBERTS, B. Dew. Mr. Bulkeley and the Pirate : a Welsh diarist of the 18th century (1936).

BOOKS IN WELSH

DAVIES, Grace G. Alawon Gwerin Mon. 2 vols. (n.d.)

EDWARDS, R. Adgofion am Llanfechell a'r cylch (1910).

EISTEDDFOD GADEIRIOL MON : cyfansoddiadau (1907 to date).

GRIFFITH, Owen. Mynydd Parys (1897).

HUGHES, Hugh. Hanes Amlwch (n.d.).

HUGHES, O. Hanes plwf Trefdraeth (1904).

HUGHES, R. Enwogion Mon (1913).

HUGHES-ROBERTS, H. Meddygon esgyrn Mon (1935).

JONES, Bobi, Crydro Mon (1957).

JONES, J. Dysgrifiad o Ynys Mon (1857).

LLOYD, O. Hynafiaethau Llanddona (1910).

OWEN, Hugh. Braslun o hanes M.C. Mon—1880–1935 (1937).

OWEN, Hugh. Hanes Plwyf Niwbwrch (1952).

PARRY, R. Enwogion Mon (1877).

PRITCHARD, J. Methodistiaid Mon, hyd 1887 (1888).

PRITCHARD, William. John Elias a'i oes (1911).

PRITCHARD, T. Hanes Sir Fon (1872).

ROBERTS, W. Trem yn old (1929).

WALKER, T. G. Dau blwyf : hanes Llangristiolus a Cherrigc einwen (c1944).

WILLIAMS, E. A. Hanes Mon yny bedwaredd ganrif a'r bymtheg (1927).

WILLIAMS, R. M. Enwogion Mon (1913).

WILLIAMS, R. T. Enwau lleoedd ym Mon (1908).

WILLIAMS, R. T. Derwyddiaeth yn Ynys Mon (1890).

WILLIAMS, R. T. Nodion o Gaergybi (1877).

Appendix (iii)

THE ALPHABET—Y WYDDOR

A B C CH D DD E F FF G NG H I L LL M N O P PH R S T TH U W Y

A GUIDE TO PRONUNCIATION

The accent in Welsh words is nearly always on the last syllable but one, except in a few instances when it falls on the last syllable. In most cases these exceptions are distinguished by the vowels being circumflexed or aspirated with 'h'.

There are no silent letters in Welsh words, and the same letter has nearly always the same sound. The letters J, K, V, X and Z do not occur in purely Welsh words.

A   short as in 'man', or long as in 'half'. Never as in 'mane'.

B   as in English.

C   as in 'can', never as in 'city'.

CH   as gutteral sound as in Scotch word 'loch', much emphasised; never sounded as in the word 'church'.

D   as in English.

*DD   has the sound of 'th' in 'this' or in 'heather', never as the 'th' in 'smith' or 'earth'.

E   as in 'men', or as 'a' in 'lady'.

F   as in 'of', or as 'v' in 'ever'.

*FF   as 'f' in 'for' or 'ff' in 'effort'.

G   always hard as 'g' in 'egg', never soft as 'g' in 'gin'.

*NG   nasal as in 'ring'.

H   always aspirated as in 'hard'.

I   short as 'i' in 'win', or long as 'ee' in 'queen'.

L   as in English.

*LL   has no equivalent sound in English, but is pronounced by placing the tip of the tongue at the back of the top teeth, and forcing out the breath on both sides of the tongue.

M   as in English.

N   as in English.

O   short as 'o' in 'not' or long as 'o' in 'rose'.

P   as in English.

*PH   as 'ph' in 'physic' (has the same sound as the Welsh 'FF').
R   always trilled as 'rr' in 'arrow' or 'r' in the French word
      'père'.
S   as in 'sin', never as in 'things'.
T   as in English.
*TH   as in 'thin'.
U   as 'y' in 'hymn'.
W   as 'oo' in 'fool'.
Y   as 'u' in 'run'; when occuring in the last syllable of words
      of more than one syllable and followed by a vowel, is
      sounded like the 'y' in 'hymn'.

*These letters, when appearing in Welsh words, are not simply
double letters, but have always the special sounds as described
above.

Welsh consonants are not difficult. Single 'L' is always per-
missible in 'Llan'; never 'thlan' or 'flan'. The 'CH' is like the
Scottish sound in 'loch' or the German 'Bach'. The single 'F'
is a 'V', as in 'of'; eisteddvod, not 'fod'. The 'DD' is simply the
Welsh form of the English soft 'TH' in 'this', 'with' and 'bathe'.
The first syllable of Beddgelert is exactly rendered by the English
'bathe', not 'bed'. All other consonants are as in English, except
that 'C' and 'G' are always hard; so is the Welsh 'S' always
hard, as in 'sea'—never soft as in 'rose', and is more heavily
stressed than in English. The aspirate is always clearly heard
in correctly spoken Welsh, both in initial and medial positions,
even after consonants such as in fy mhen (my head).

SOME TOPOGRAPHICAL TERMS

Aber	—Mouth (of river)	Llyn	—Lake
Afon	—River	Maes	—Stone
Bach	—Small	Maen	—Field
Bro	—Vale	Mawr	—Large
Bryn	—Hill	Mor	—Sea
Bwlch	—Pass	Mynydd	—Mountain
Cader	—Fortress	Pen	—Head
Cwm	}—Valley	Pentre	—Village
Dyffryn		Rhiw	—Hill
Dinas	—City (of fortress)	Rhyd	—Ford
Eglwys	—Church	Sant	—Saint
Glan	—Shore	Traeth	—Beach
Llan	—Church	Tre	—Town

EXAMPLES OF PLACE-NAME PRONUNCIATION

Amlwch	—Amlooch
Camaes	—Kemmyse
Llandysilio	—Lan-duss-ilyo
Menai	—Menn-eye
Rhosneigr	—Rose-neygger
Llangefni	—Lan-gevny
Llanerchymedd	—Lannerhrch-er-maythe
Moelfre	—Moyl-vray
Penmaenmawr	—Penmyne-ma-oor
Y Wyddfa	—Err Withfa (Snowdon)

COUNTIES OF WALES — SIROEDD CYMRU

Anglesey	Sir Fôn
Brecknockshire	Sir Frycheiniog
Caernarvonshire	Sir Gaernarfon
Cardiganshire	Sir Aberteifi
Carmarthenshire	Sir Gaerfyrddin
Denbighshire	Sir Ddinbych
Flintshire	Sir Fflint
Glamorganshire	Sir Forgannwg
Merionethshire	Sir Feirionnydd
Montgomeryshire	Sir Drefaldwyn
Pembrokeshire	Sir Benfro
Radnorshire	Sir Faesyfed

(The 'I' is long in 'sir' as 'EE' in 'queen'.)

CARDINAL NUMBERS — RHIFAU ARBENNIG

One	Un
Two	Dau (f. dwy)
Three	Tri (f. tair)
Four	Pedwar (f. pedair)
Five	Pump (pum when preceding a noun, e.g. pum dyn)
Six	Chwech
Seven	Saith
Eight	Wyth
Nine	Naw
Ten	Deg

Eleven	Un-ar-ddeg
Twelve	Deuddeg
Hundred	Cant
Thousand	Mil
Million	Miliwn

(f.—feminine)

MONEY	ARIAN
Farthing	Ffyrling
Halfpenny	Dimai
One penny	Geiniog
Threepence	Tair ceiniog
Sixpence	Chwecheiniog
Shilling	Swllt
Two shillings	Dau swllt
Half-a-crown	Hanner-coron
Ten shillings	Deg swllt
Pound	Punt
Five pounds	Pum punt
TIME	AMSER
A second	Eiliad
Seconds	Eiliadau
A minute	Munud
Minutes	Munudau
An hour	Awr
Hours	Oriau
A day	Dydd
Days	Dyddiau
A week	Wythnos
Weeks	Wythnosau
A fortnight	Pythefnos
A month	Mis
Months	Misoedd
A year	Blwyddyn
Years	Blynyddoedd
Morning	Bore
Noon (Mid-day)	Canol-dydd
Afternoon	Prynhawn
Evening	Hwyr
Night	Nos

ACKNOWLEDGEMENTS

The author gratefully acknowledges the following publishers, writers and photographers whose books and works have been of invaluable help in the preparation of this book, particularly where kind permission was granted to quote from copyright material:

A Book of Wales, by D. M. & E. M. Lloyd (Collins); The Land of Wales, by Eiluned & Peter Lewis (Batsford); A History of Mona, by Angharad Llwyd; Royal Commission on Ancient and Historic Monuments (H.M.S.O.); Memoirs of the Geological Survey, by Edward Greenly (H.M.S.O.); Anglesey Antiquarian Society & Field Club Transactions (Gwenlyn Evans, Caernarvon); Social Life in Mid-Eighteenth Century Anglesey, and Religion & Politics in Mid-Eighteenth Century Anglesey, both by Lady G. Nesta Evans; Anglesey and North Wales Coast, by F. H. Glazebrook (Brookland & Co., Bangor); Mr. Bulkeley and the Pirate, by B. Dew Roberts (Oxford University Press); The Holyhead Road, by Charles G. Harper (Chapman & Hall); The Chester and Holyhead Railway, by J. M. Dunn (Oakwood Press); Welsh Fairy Tales and Other Stories, and Tales from Welsh Wales, both by P. H. Emerson (D. Nutt); From Hand to Hand, by T. Rowland Hughes (by permission of Colonel Richard Ruck and Methuen & Co.); The Complete Poems of W. H. Davies (by permission of Mrs. Davies and Jonathan Cape Ltd.).

The old copper trading harbour at Amlwch.

Not snow—but blown sand in Môn Forest. A constant battle is waged by the Forestry Commission to stabilise a desert of shifting sand big enough at times to bury homes.

Endpiece

A PROPHECY

In the morning in Anglesey I arose,
and straight for my journey prepared;
In Chester I first broke my fast,
In noon in green Erin I dined,
And evening beheld me in Mona,
Enjoying my own turf fireside.

Robin Dhu's Prophecy, 1340.

Index

INDEX

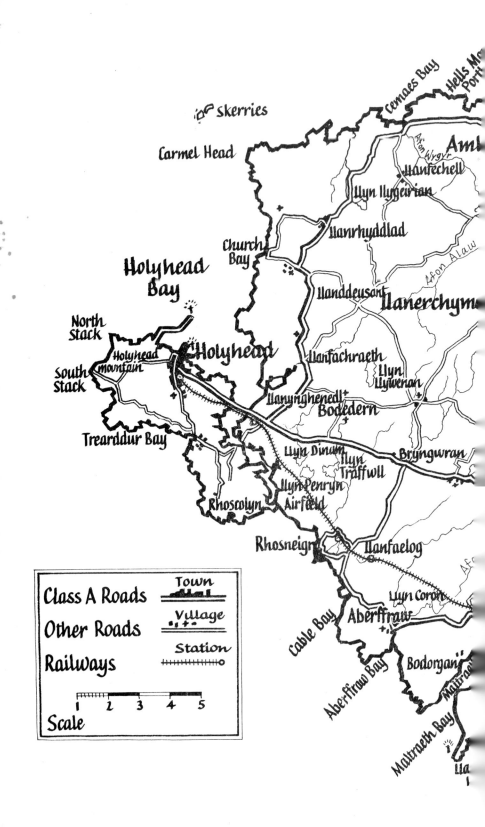